As a mother of nine children and many grandchildren, Myra J. Martinez, has much experience in the challenges of motherhood. She has also endured much suffering with her oldest child's childhood cancer while raising a large family.

She enjoys cooking, spending time with and entertaining her large family. She has also taken her experience to the Gospel of Life Disciples, where she spends time loving, comforting, ministering, and praying with those who are dying. She lives in Oklahoma, married to her grade school sweetheart, Philip, and their growing family.

Myra J. Martinez

DANIELLE

A Story of Surrender and Trust

AUSTIN MACAULEY PUBLISHERS™

LONDON • CAMBRIDGE • NEW YORK • SHARJAH

Ordering Information
Quantity sales: Special discounts are available on quantity purchases by corporations, associations, and others. For details, contact the publisher at the address below.

Publisher's Cataloging-in-Publication data
Martinez, Myra J.
Danielle

ISBN 9798889101161 (Paperback)
ISBN 9798889101178 (ePub e-book)

Library of Congress Control Number: 2023919261

www.austinmacauley.com/us

First Published 2024
Austin Macauley Publishers LLC
40 Wall Street, 33rd Floor, Suite 3302
New York, NY 10005
USA

mail-usa@austinmacauley.com
+1 (646) 5125767

A special thank you to my husband, Philip, who helped tremendously in putting in hours of his time proofreading a story that I know was extremely painful for him to read over and over again.

Also, a special thanks to my close family, friends, and catholic priests who kept praying for me and encouraging me to finish my book. If I had not had that continued encouragement, I probably would have given up on writing a long time ago.

I truly appreciate the Editor Production Department, especially, Jessica Bosak at Austin Macauley Publications for making my book to the public possible.

Most of all I thank God for giving me the courage and strength to be able to relive my experiences and turn my thought into words. I know on my own, without God's help that never would have been possible.

Table of Contents

Introduction

I have felt that I have been called to write and share about my faith experiences and our family's difficult time of suffering regarding my first of nine children, Danielle. She suffered for two and a half years from Acute Lymphatic Leukemia and died on 1 January 1995, at the beautiful age of seven. I am hopeful, that by the grace of God, our story can possibly help other people find peace, purpose, and acceptance in their own suffering. It is my heart's desire that her story will not only present the beauty of faith in a child's life, but also that there is sweetness to be found in suffering and even in death. It is only by the good grace of our Lord, through the Holy Spirit, I am even able to recall Danielle's life in a way that will hopefully be a gift and inspiration to others in their faith journey. Many people did not know the beauty in Danielle's soul until after her death.

While Danielle was living, I kept to myself many of the special things about her life. I feel Danielle was a very beautiful soul, and hope that by coming to know her, others who are called to suffer will be inspired. Danielle was never able to witness big miracles but she always kept a strong faith and a deep love for Jesus in her heart even through her most tremendous suffering. She was especially close to her

Confirmation patron saint, St. Therese of Lisieux, who gave her a beautiful example of faith. Danielle trusted and did not need to visibly see or witness a miracle, to know God was always with her, by her side, at every instance. She was also very aware of her Guardian Angel friend and believed he was with her at all times, helping her, and watching over her. She prayed daily with our family, the 'Guardian Angel' prayer. She loved learning about her Catholic faith, especially the angels and the saints. She definitely found her peace and strength to suffer through her faith in Jesus, and that was something as a mother I could not give.

I have asked Danielle to pray for me while I am writing these details of her short life. I pray God will help me find joy in my writings, instead of great suffering. Danielle's life was short but filled with goodness. I am trusting the Holy Spirit to help me do my best to recall all the important details about Danielle's life so I may share them with you, and they may hopefully touch your soul.

It is to all who suffer, I come
to confide and share the story of little
Danielle Nichole Therese Martinez

I pray the Holy Spirit will inspire my
writings and give me the strength to
endure them.

Together at Last

Sometimes, people hear stories about children who fall in love and grow up to be married in spite of all the odds against them. Well, my life was like one of those fairy tale relationships. When I was eleven and in the sixth grade, there was a cute Hispanic basketball boy named Philip in the eighth grade at my grade school. The private school was small and I had a cousin in that class, who was good friends with Philip, so we had connections. Philip only knew me as David's little blonde-haired and blued-eyed cousin. One day, a mutual friend of ours called Philip and asked him who he thought the prettiest girl was in the sixth grade. Philip told her, "Myra." So, as a joke, they came up with the idea of asking me to 'go steady' with him. It would be a joke because they knew I was very shy and it would embarrass me. Besides, I was so much younger. This was to be a cruel joke to me, but I made it backfire on him by saying, "Yes." He was not expecting this at all. Oddly enough, as time went on, our relationship grew and blossomed to the beautiful point of marriage.

After what felt like a very long wait, our lives joined together on 10 January 1987, when Philip and I were married. On our wedding day, I was so excited and could not wait to spend the rest of my life with my very best friend! I never had a doubt in my mind Philip and I should be together forever. Some people made remarks I had made a mistake of not dating other men, but I had no desire, for I felt in my heart Philip was definitely the one I wanted by my side until I die. He was my first and only love. Even though this long-term relationship worked out for us, it is not something I would recommend. I felt God must have played a part in all of this, since we met in such an unusual manner. The Holy Spirit surely had a special plan for us both and our future children.

Our wedding took place at St. Andrew's Catholic Church in Moore, Oklahoma. Fr George Pupius was the celebrant. We spent a great deal of time and preparation planning the big wedding. All the songs and readings for the Mass were chosen by us to reflect the theme of our wedding, which was, 'God Lives in our Love'. A few hundred people came to share in our celebration, and later, many were there to help us in times to come. We were blessed to have come from such a supportive and caring community.

Both Philip and I were the youngest members of our families. When we married, Philip was twenty-one and I was only nineteen.

We had both always lived at home with our parents until the day of our marriage. The following day, we began our lives together in Ballwin, MO (a suburb of St. Louis) while Philip attended Logan College of chiropractic and I began a new job working for an insurance company. We lived in St. Louis for the next three and a half years until Philip's school was complete. Honestly, the first two weeks together were not easy.

Not only did we have to get used to living with each other, but we had the challenge of being separated from our families. Living those days with no cell phones was especially challenging. Every time our apartment phone rang, we both raced to see who could get there first, laughing and pushing each other all the way. Even though we had each other, it was still very lonely at times. Now, when I look back on it, if we had stronger faith, we would have had more peace and comfort. We attended mass every Sunday and we prayed some, but we had a lot of room to learn and grow. We were very much lacking as the couple God needed us to be. Over the years, through a combination of the Sacraments of the Church, sacrifices, prayer, and spiritual reading, we have been given many graces that have helped us to continue to grow and develop a deeper loving relationship with the Lord. The true goal of marriage is for each spouse to help get the other to Heaven, our final home. We have found faith to be a continuous growing process.

An Unexpected Joy

Within a month of our marriage, we were faced with our first challenge. Since we were new to the methods of natural family planning and the excitement of finally being married, I quickly became pregnant with our first child. For those of great faith, this would not be as big of a challenge, but for us, who were still very immature in our faith, it seemed as though our little world had come to an end. We later discovered it was not at all the end. It was, in fact, the beginning of a beautiful life and the first of many blessings!

At the time we discovered I was pregnant, there were very mixed emotions, one of which was being scared. I was never overly worried about our financial needs or Philip's schooling as much as I was nervous about the unknown. It did not take very long for me to get excited; after all, I was going to have a baby! I had always envisioned myself having about four or five children and staying home with them. I must have started those feelings very early in my life because when I was a child, I loved playing for hours with my baby dolls. Since I had no sisters, it was my dolls who had to keep me company. I guess God was already training me for my future calling to be a mother. I never, even for a day, dreamed of having a big career. I always only thought of myself as being a nun or a stay-at-home mom. I feel I was blessed to know my calling at an early age.

For Philip, it was quite different. He thought it would be impossible to finish Chiropractic College. Sadly, he was not as excited and could only think of the financial difficulties this would bring and that his dream of becoming a chiropractor since the age of thirteen appeared to be shattered. Philip consulted with several of his classmates who had children to see how they were coping financially and mentally with balancing school and a family. They gave some encouraging advice for him, but still Philip felt unsure. Then, one Sunday, while at mass, the priest gave an inspirational homily that changed his whole attitude. He came home after church and was prepared to have twins! The Holy Spirit had worked in a powerful way.

Fortunately, God gave us much grace to overcome this first trial in our married lives. With the passing of time, the pregnancy became very joyful and exciting for us both.

We began looking forward to the birth of our first child. I began trying really hard to take care of myself. I began eating healthier, walking daily, and spent a lot of time searching for a suitable obstetrician. The doctor not only had to be good, but most importantly, needed to be pro-life. I also began praying for our baby and for a safe delivery.

On many occasions before my baby was born, I offered my child totally to God. I usually made this offering of consecration on Sundays after receiving Jesus in the Holy Eucharist knowing when I received Him, my baby was receiving as well. I asked God to use my child however He needed to do His will, even if it meant separation.

Sometimes, it would cause quiet tears to well up in my eyes and roll down my face because I did not know in what way God would choose to use my offering. I imagined that perhaps God would call my child to be a missionary nun or priest. I felt it possible that he/she might have to move to a faraway country where I would never see them. Even though I had these feelings and emotions, my heart was still willing to let go and offer my unborn child totally and completely to God. I always felt strong and good about my offerings. Though it was difficult, I felt a real sense of peace and happiness.

On one occasion at night, I had a very powerful and unusual dream, which is a bit difficult to describe. In the dream, I had a vision of Jesus coming down from heaven and touching me. A very beautiful and strange feeling came over me. Then, it was as if I felt myself rising up as I watched Jesus ascend back into heaven. I awoke with a jolt. It was not at all like a nightmare, instead it was very peaceful and joyful. After waking, I had a very beautiful and warm feeling of happiness. The only sense I could make of it all was believing Jesus was blessing the little baby I carried in a very special way.

Four weeks before my due date, I went to work as if it were any other day. That evening, Philip and I went for our daily walk together. I really miss those simple days when I think about them and I'll cherish them always. Later in the evening, we attended our natural birthing class where we practiced pushing and breathing techniques. I sometimes wonder if the classes of pushing were responsible for starting my labor that very night, because a few hours after returning home, my water broke and my labor began prematurely. Since my labor was four weeks premature and this was our first baby, we were both very nervous. Philip stayed calm and was very helpful to me. I was so scared about the baby coming so soon and so unexpectedly. Thankfully, it was in the early hours of the night, so traffic was not bad. We silently prayed as we drove thirty minutes to St. John's Mercy Health Center in St. Louis. The prayers helped calm our nerves and gave us a sense of peace. I was fortunate to have a short labor of three and a half hours.

On 17 September 1987, I delivered a seven pound three ounce baby girl! We had no idea if the baby would be a boy or girl. We spent the whole pregnancy thinking the baby was a boy, so we were really surprised! We named our new healthy baby girl, Danielle Nichole. She was a perfectly beautiful baby with a dark complexion and very thick black hair. Philip and I were blessed with a precious gift from God and we were very excited and thankful.

Our Hearts Are So Full

Shortly after Danielle was born, I quit my job at an insurance company, where I worked and stayed home full time to be with Danielle. This really was no sacrifice for me and a decision I will never regret. I soaked up every precious moment I was at home with her and loved experiencing every first move she made.

A week after Danielle was born, I began a nine-day novena to St. Therese of Lisieux. This saint would eventually play a large part in Danielle's life. In my novena, I prayed Danielle would always love God and be very close and pleasing to Him. It is a custom when praying with St. Therese to ask for a rose as a sign of answered prayer. At the end of my novena, I received a handmade baby blanket as a gift for Danielle. The small blanket was covered in sweet pink rosebuds. I gladly took this rose blanket as a sign my prayers for Danielle had been heard. When Danielle was in kindergarten, she used to take this same blanket to school to cover herself at nap time. It is something special I cherish very dearly.

On 11 October 1987, when Danielle was three weeks old, she received the Sacrament of Baptism in Ballwin, Missouri, at Holy Infant Catholic Church, by Fr Robert

Rosebrough. She wore a long beautiful white satin and lace dress I purchased with a fifty-dollar savings bond my grandmother left for me when she died. All of my daughters were baptized in this same dress. Her uncle, Joe Martinez, was her godfather and my very close and beloved friend, Dolores Person, was her godmother. Both godparents came to St. Louis for the baptism, along with Philip's parents and other family members. It was a beautiful and holy day! We were all very happy to celebrate the baptism of little Danielle Nichole Martinez. This became the beginning of a life dedicated to God.

Throughout her infancy, I continued praying for Danielle and offering her to God. It seemed she was under frequent attack. When she was four months old, she experienced the first threat to her life. While shopping with me, Danielle was getting a little fussy, so I gave her a box out of the cart to play with. At this time, she had no teeth but she was gnawing on the box.

Danielle had chewed off a small piece of the cardboard box and started choking and began gasping for air. I began to get frightened and was getting ready to cry for help when I put my finger into her mouth to see if I could reach the object. This caused her to gag and she threw up the cardboard piece. After everything, she was fine, and I was extremely relieved. As my legs were shaking, I thanked God and His Holy angels for saving her life. Later in the day, when I was telling my mom about the event, she had an addition to the story. She said while she was in the church parking lot getting ready to attend mass, she noticed the brown scapular hanging on the rear-view mirror of her car had suddenly come off and fell into her lap. Thinking that was unusual, she took this as a sign that we needed prayer. As she continued, I asked her about what time this happened and it was exactly the same time Danielle was choking.

I always thought Danielle was a very easy baby. She never had colic, was enjoyable to be around, very attentive, and mostly content. Teaching the faith began early. Before she could talk or walk, I began teaching her about Jesus and Mary. I used to pray very simple prayers with her, such as, saying, "Jesus, I love you!" or, "Thank you, God for this day!" and other short praises. I also frequently sang to her religious songs. I would show her a crucifix or a holy picture and tell her who they were. I traced her with the sign of the cross often. Because of this, Danielle could recognize pictures of Jesus and Mary at an early age. She loved to kiss the crucifix and would hug her unbreakable statue of Mary holding the Infant Jesus. She would always smile when she looked at them. Sometimes, we would find her staring into an empty corner of the room and laughing. Her attention would be held there for several minutes at a time and this would always fascinate us. We often wondered if she was allowed to see her Guardian Angel when she was a baby. Who knows? But it's a beautiful wonder.

On one occasion, while at mass, Danielle was being cranky and fussy. Nothing could settle her down. When it was getting closer to the time to receive Communion and I began to get distressed because I really wanted to receive Communion but couldn't see how I could possibly go since Danielle was crying so hard. I began praying to my Guardian Angel, asking for his assistance. I had hoped maybe he could help keep her quiet and bring her peace. Right after my prayer was finished, a woman whom I had never met, came up to us and asked if she could hold Danielle for me while I went to Communion. Without any reservation, I said, "Yes." Keep in mind, this was my first child and I had no clue who this woman was, but I felt peace about it. As soon as I handed Danielle to the woman, she stopped crying. It was like an instant peace for both of us. I can't help but think my angel had answered my prayer. He sent this woman from church to help us. It is not every day a stranger comes up to you and asks if she can hold your baby during mass. The angel let this kind woman feel my distress and she happily came to my assistance.

Danielle began growing up to be a very bright little girl. She began talking at a very early age. By the time she was thirteen months old, she was speaking in sentences, and at eighteen months, she spoke clearly in paragraphs. Before her second birthday, she could recite and recognize all upper- and lower-case letters in the alphabet. She also knew all the shapes and colors. She was very happy and loved to laugh! She had the thickest, curly brown hair and chubby cheeks. We loved her so much. Our hearts were full.

Growing in Faith

When Danielle was about seven months old, I found myself pregnant for the second time. I went to a pro-life pregnancy support service called Birthright for help. The volunteer there was very kind and assured me that having another baby was not the end of the world; rather, a blessing and eased my mind after speaking with her. I was very familiar with this organization because my mother had been a long-time volunteer in Oklahoma City. That non-profit organization is known for free pregnancy testing, helping pregnant women with free counseling and lots of love.

Again, for us, it did not seem like the perfect timing, but once again, God was in control and had a plan greater than ours. He sent us this second soul to care for and we just needed to trust Him. Sadly, many people were unhappy about the pregnancy, even close family members. They felt we were crazy having another baby while Philip was still in college. So many times, we had to suffer hearing comments, such as, 'That's all you need now! Don't you know what causes that?' While I'm sure they did not mean to hurt us, the lack of support did cause us suffering, but this time we trusted God more. We knew, He really blessed us with Danielle and this child would also be another beautiful blessing. Once again, God was in control with a wonderful plan. He just needed our abandonment and trust.

Physically, my body was a bit stressed having two babies so close together. I continued to breast feed Danielle through the pregnancy, which wore on me, making me more tired. It was very difficult to continue nursing, but I was thankful I was still able to give Danielle the closeness she needed as a baby. Offering these kinds of sufferings as sacrifices to God and making them a prayer started to become a habit for me since it seemed I was given many opportunities. I was always learning. I found that making sacrifices only brought me closer to Jesus and helped me survive those nursing and exhausting days. Philip was not available much to help since he was at school in the day, spent his evenings studying, and working a part-time job. I was really missing my family and the help I would have had in Oklahoma City. It was very difficult being so far away from my mother and not having her love and support. Unfortunately, we only talked every couple of weeks, since using a telephone was a long-distance call costing money.

Early in this second pregnancy, I was holding Danielle, and tripped on one of her toys in our living room. Unfortunately, I broke my arm and ended up in a cast for six long weeks. Ironically, I had been praying and asking God to give me suffering in my life so I could offer my sufferings as a prayer and grow closer to Him. Since then, I have learned, it is really not necessary to ask for suffering. God gives it in His time when He feels a person can handle it; therefore, there is really no need to ask. The sufferings I experienced were not just physical pain, but I also had to step out of the caregiving role for Danielle. I could not fold clothes, give Danielle her bath, and many other daily tasks. Fortunately, Philip adapted to these new responsibilities with Danielle and it strengthened their relationship.

During this pregnancy, I kept feeling a strong desire to become closer to our Lord. I wanted to do something for Him, but I was unsure what it would be. All my life, I had a desire to grow more in my faith, but I had come to a time in my life where I was starting to become stronger in virtue and grow spiritually. I missed volunteering as I did in my high school Key Club. That group gave me opportunities and experiences to help work with mentally handicap children, orphans, and visit nursing homes. I really enjoyed being able to assist them and hoped I could find something similar. I called the church office and spoke to our parish priest about my desire to do something more. He invited Danielle and me to come with him once a week to mass and visit elderly Catholics in a nearby nursing home. I did and enjoyed this very much!

I felt Danielle's chubby cheeks and smiling baby face brought a lot of happiness to these people, some who suffered horribly from loneliness. Throughout my life after this I had thought I would like to visit the sick and help them in some way again. About 29 years later, I finally found a special deep calling to volunteer for the Gospel of Life Disciples+Dwellings. At the Dwellings, we welcome those who would otherwise be alone and accompany them on the journey toward eternal life. I minister to the dying at John Paul II Dwelling in Moore, Oklahoma. It is here I have found joy and peace knowing I am being called to such a special place to bring love, companionship and prayer to the elderly, the sick and the dying.

God continued to call me to serve Him and love Him in other ways. It was in the summer of 1988, when God sent a beautiful holy woman into my life. Danielle and I spent a lot of time at the neighborhood swimming pool down the street from our condominium. It was there I met Diane, and her little girl, Caitlin. After talking with Diane, we discovered we not only shared the same Catholic faith, but we had been attending the same Holy Infant Catholic Church. Diane told me that she belonged to a Blue Army Prayer Cell. It was a group of mothers who gathered each week with their children to pray the rosary for priests. Diane invited me to meet her at early morning mass and I could follow her to the prayer cell. I jumped at the invitation and said yes! I was still burning with a desire to do something more for the Lord. I felt this was just what I needed in my life, a friend who would really help lead me closer to Christ and help me grow in my faith. My prayers were being answered.

Danielle was a late sleeper, so making it to the 8:00 a.m. morning mass was quite a challenge, but God gave me the will and determination. Also, the night before, I asked my guardian angel to help Danielle and me to wake up and give us a less hectic morning. With the extra help from above, we were able to manage to be there on time. Diane was really happy to see that I had made it to Mass. The prayer cell turned out to be a wonderful and very spiritual experience. These holy mothers were such an inspiration to me. They were instrumental in my continual road of conversion. I already knew how to pray the rosary, but they introduced me to many new things, such as examples and ideas on how to teach my children the faith. They taught me how to be more like the Blessed Mother. They were such beautiful, holy examples and I am eternally grateful.

At this time, I was only twenty-one. The next youngest person in the prayer cell was about thirty. Though I felt very young, I always felt comfortable with them. The beautiful thing about it was, no matter what our differences were, we all had the common bond of our Catholic faith and motherhood. We all shared the same goals and the same desires. I believe the single-most important thing to all of us was forming the souls of our children and helping them get to Heaven. Raising our children for God was our common bond. We all believed our children's souls were more important than any worldly desires. I would rather my child have a belief and great love for our Lord, than to have a child brilliant and educated who knows nothing of God. The soul is so much more precious and important than the intellect, and life is short, but Heaven is for all eternity. I was beginning to learn motherhood is an incredible vocation from God. I learned I could serve God in a very full way by caring for my children in whom He dwells and teaching them a faith that brings them close to Him. My ultimate goal in life has always been to help get my children to Heaven and will always be my number one goal.

Then There Were Two

About two months before my second child was due, I began having a lot of contractions. Again, it looked like I was going to have another baby prematurely for some unknown reason. I was put on medication and told to stay off my feet as much as possible. This bed rest might sound like a nice break, but being told to lay in bed for a long time is another way to suffer. I have never cared for television, so I spent most of my time praying and reading religious books. I love to learn more about my Catholic faith, so I tried to make the experience somewhat of a spiritual retreat. I had to rely on my husband Philip to do most of the housework and caring for Danielle.

During this second pregnancy, we were met with another challenge. A small lump was discovered in Danielle's genital area. She was taken to the doctor and on 2 December 1988; she was diagnosed with an inguinal hernia. We were told she needed surgery to have it repaired. That following Sunday, Danielle received the Sacrament of the Sick for the first time in her life. A lot of people began praying for Danielle for the surgery to go well. I was concerned about her, but I was not afraid. I felt a hernia was not too serious, though it did add extra stress in our life and on my pregnancy.

On 13 December 1988, Danielle had her first surgery. My mother came to help us and be a support. The surgery took a little longer than expected, which caused us great concern. When the doctor came out, we were told she did not have a hernia, but an internal hemangioma. This was a mass of blood vessels that proliferated in a single area. The doctor removed it and it was confirmed to be a benign mass.

After the surgery, it hurt so much to see Danielle with an IV in her little hand. She was crying and was too little to understand what was happening. This would only be a little taste of the suffering we would endure in the future. I remember being pregnant and nursing her while she was in the recovery room. I could tell all the added stress was causing me a lot more contractions and I was still five weeks from my baby's due date.

Danielle recovered well from the surgery, but all the excitement had an effect on my pregnancy.

Three days following the surgery, on 16 December 1988, I began premature labor. This was a hard time because all of our friends had gone out of town for the holidays and there was no one to care for Danielle. My mother had just gone back to Oklahoma City. Our only option was to take Danielle to the hospital with us and hoped she would not be a problem. It was late at night and the temperature was 11 degrees outside. We had to wake Danielle from her sleep and carry her to a car that we prayed would start. Danielle must have understood she was about to become a big sister because she seemed so excited.

One hour after arriving at the hospital, I delivered a healthy baby girl! However, it wasn't without challenges. We had to ask the nurse to watch Danielle so Philip could go into the delivery room. He had to come in and out so he could keep checking on Danielle. This left me without a birthing coach. Without a birthing coach, my breathing became too fast and I started to hyperventilate. I kept telling the nurses my arms were tingling and becoming numb. At first, they were ignoring me because they were more concerned that the doctor had not shown up yet. After continuous complaining, they finally gave me some oxygen, which gave me immediate relief and saved me from passing out. Unfortunately, the doctor was not quick enough and our new little girl came before he arrived. It was a little scary, but everything was fine. I always teased Philip that someday he might have to deliver one of our children. I am happy to say I was always blessed to have short labors.

We named our healthy baby girl, Dominique Noel, after St. Dominic. Since the rosary had become such an important part of my life, and Mary gave the rosary to St. Dominic, I felt it would be appropriate. I also thought the name was beautiful, it meant 'Belonging to God'. Just as I consecrated Danielle to God before she was born, I had consecrated Dominique to the Immaculate Heart of Mary. Now even as an adult, Dominique continues to have a devotion to the Blessed Mother, the rosary, and always wears the Miraculous Medal.

It was really hard staying in St. Louis that Christmas. We missed our families so much. We also missed sharing our newborn baby with them. It was a great time of joy, but it was also a very lonely time for us. Since, Philip was out of school for Christmas break, he was able to take care of Danielle, Dominique, and me.

Danielle was so proud of her new little sister, Dominique. She never really showed any signs of jealousy. She accepted her new baby sister with open arms. The girls were to become very best friends. There was never a need to worry when I left Danielle alone in a room with her baby sister; I could always trust her. She treated her gently, just as she did her baby doll. She loved to pat and kiss Dominique. She did not have a problem sharing my lap or my affection.

When Dominique was born, Danielle was only fifteen months old and had just begun to walk; therefore, when we went out, I had to carry both the girls. This made attending daily mass even more difficult. We lived in a third-floor condominium, so I also struggled to carry both girls down the stairs myself. I would carry Danielle in my left arm and my other arm held the baby carrier with Dominique. Even the walk across the parking lot seemed to be quite a struggle. I had to pray just to make it to the front door! I used to offer this struggle up as a small sacrifice to God. I felt the graces I would receive for attending mass with such a challenge would be far greater than attending mass without such complications.

Sometimes, Danielle would fight with Dominique, as siblings do, but when it came to other children, Danielle was always kind. She was even good to those who hurt her. When other children would hit or pinch her, she would cry, but she never hurt them back. This kindness and love for others was something she would never lose. Some might have seen her as passive or weak but, in fact, I believe it was her faith and love for Jesus that gave her a kind and gentle spirit. Since she was very little, she would often state how she loved everyone in the whole world. Danielle emulated the loving forgiveness of Jesus well. Love everyone and treat all with kindness has always been my motto in teaching my children.

Going Home: A Family of Five

When Danielle was two and Dominique six months, I found myself in an unexpected pregnancy once again. We were still living in St. Louis and Philip was in his last trimester of Chiropractic College.

This time people criticized us even more than before. No one seemed to be happy or excited about this new little life, except a few close family members and my mother. One of Philip's classmates even made the comment we should be concerned about overpopulation. A lot of people felt we were irresponsible and careless, including those from our church and our families. This made it even more hurtful. So many people would ask us how many more children we planned on having. We would simply answer them in a way they did not understand by saying, "We will have as many as God gives us." They never quite knew how to respond to that. Of course, all of this did make it hard on us, and unfortunately, I was not very humble and hated telling people of the pregnancy, for fear of what they would say or what they might think. I did not want to be judged. Despite all of the counseling people gave us on artificial birth control, we felt confident we were living our lives for God and everything was all in God's special plans. We had to put our whole life in His hands and surrender ourselves to Him. It required a great deal of faith and trust in the Lord. Only God knew what was best for us, and evidently He knew having another baby, at that time, was a wonderful blessing.

Again, I was faced with another difficult pregnancy. Just as before, two months before my due date, I was put on medication and complete bed rest to slow my contractions, since I was already beginning to threaten premature labor. With Danielle and Dominique being so small, this was very hard to do. Philip had to go to school, so he was not able to help during the day, but he was there to help in the evenings. I know these hard times were very difficult for him. He not only had to study, but he had to fix dinner, change diapers, bathe the girls and help get them to bed at night. God really blessed me with a wonderful, helpful husband who is very sacrificial. I couldn't have survived without him. He has always been very helpful. I guess it would be appropriate to call Philip my 'Simon at Calvary', because whenever I had a cross too heavy to carry alone, he was there to help me carry it. It was a cross we carried together as a couple.

My friends from the prayer cell rosary group were also very helpful. They would kindly come over and spend the day helping me care for the girls. They were generous and happy to help. One friend told me it reminded her of the visitation, when the Blessed Mother took care of Elizabeth during her pregnancy. She said caring for us was like the rosary coming to life for her. I will always remember this. It helps me a lot when I see others in need of my help. Besides these women, I also had other good friends who lived in the condominium complex who made meals for us and sometimes watched my girls. Everyone was so helpful! It was very touching and much appreciated. They inspired me to always do my best to reach out to others who are in need.

This bed rest time was difficult. I missed going to mass and caring for my family. I never thought I would miss the laundry or changing diapers, but I really did. When the girls would get hurt, they started going to their daddy more and more for attention. I found them detaching from me because they had less need for me, therefore, I felt useless. I offered this up to God once again and made my suffering a living prayer and united myself with the cross. This relieved the weight a little and helped me cope. Fortunately, this struggling time was short.

On 23 January 1990, we had a healthy beautiful baby girl! We named her Gabrielle Angelica, after the Angel Gabriel. I had been studying about angels throughout my pregnancy and grew in my love for them. Gabrielle's name meant, 'God is my strength'. Before her birth, I consecrated her to the angels. Even though Gabrielle was four weeks premature, we came home from the hospital the next day. The timing of Gabrielle's birth was actually perfect. Philip was getting ready to graduate from Logan College of Chiropractic and we planned to move back to Oklahoma City to be near our family whom we had missed so much.

Getting Settled in
Our New Home

One month after Gabrielle was born, we moved back to Oklahoma City. Danielle was very excited about living near her grandparents, aunts, uncles, and cousins. Having family around is something we all missed very much! We stayed with my parents for a couple of weeks until we could find a house to rent. Finally, a house was found. Philip was working for a chiropractor in North Oklahoma City and the house was not far away. Times were pretty tough for a while with three little girls running around and our income was barely enough to pay Philip's large student loans and our normal living expenses. Needless to say, my days of daily masses had come to a complete stop for a while. I offered this up as a sacrifice I would have to make. I knew the day would come when I would again be able to attend daily Mass, but at that time things were just too difficult.

I really began to miss community prayer. I felt lost without my Blue Army Prayer Cell in St. Louis. I began feeling the Holy Spirit strongly calling me to start my own rosary cenacle. I was always kind of shy and not overly confident; therefore, starting something on my own took great effort. I prayed a lot about this decision. At the time, we belonged to the parish of St. Charles Borromeo in North Oklahoma City. One day, I got brave and decided to take the girls with me up to the church and introduce myself. I hoped to find out if there was a need for a rosary group. I spoke with a very kind woman named Joanne who told me my idea sounded very good. She allowed me to print a message in the church bulletin. I invited all mothers and children interested in joining a weekly prayer cenacle to contact me. Since I had become knowledgeable about the Marian Movement of Priests cenacles, I decided their prayer format would be very good.

I received a response from the bulletin, but it was not as good as I had hoped. We began to meet weekly, praying the rosary with our children. I continued to offer our rosaries for priests. We had about four or five women and their children attending the cenacle which took place in a room at the church. I continued leading this cenacle faithfully until we moved to a new parish on the south side of town. After I left, that prayer cenacle discontinued.

Also during this time, I was trying to lead my family in a deeper understanding and relationship with God. On 6 August 1990, on the Feast of the Transfiguration, we had our home Enthroned to the Sacred Heart of Jesus. This took a lot of prayer and preparation. We had a mass celebrated in our home by our parish priest, Fr Paul Gallitin. We asked Jesus to be King of our home and family.

We consecrated our family to the Sacred Heart of Jesus and to the Immaculate Heart of Mary. In the process of the Enthronement, we accepted twelve promises of the Sacred Heart given to St. Margaret Mary.

The first few of these promises dealt with God's mercy. This was a preparation for things to come because we were never promised we would not suffer, but we were promised peace and grace during our trials and tribulations. We are so grateful we had our home Enthroned to the Sacred Heart! I highly recommend Home Enthronement to all families who want to grow more in their faith and recognize, in a more spiritual way, Jesus as the King of their hearts and home. At a minimum, I would highly recommend a house blessing for every home. All homes and families need the peace and protection only Jesus can give.

In October of 1990, when our children were three, two and ten months old, we began a major adventure in our lives. Philip quit his job as an associate chiropractor and we moved to South Oklahoma City where we started our own chiropractic practice. This was a very big decision for us and required much thought and prayer. In order to survive, we had to take out a large loan from the bank. We were already in a great deal of debt from student loans, so we knew taking out a large business loan would be very risky and require great trust in God to provide for our family. We had to have a co-signer from Philip's parents. Cuts had to be made in our financial budgets. One major change was canceling our health insurance. We thought the worst thing that could happen was a broken bone, so Philip had an x-ray machine, and he had contacts for orthopedic help. This seemed like a safe decision since none of the kids had any illnesses for the past two years. Philip had the loan proposal ready in a month's time and an office space was located.

Fortunately, with family connections, and the help of divine intervention, everything fell into place. The Martinez Chiropractic Clinic was opened on 1 November 1990.

As expected, times were really rough for us the first eight months. Then Philip was presented an opportunity which we thought would help. It was another 'trusting in God' decision. He bought a chiropractic practice an hour and a half away in Sulphur, Oklahoma. It was already established and had a good patient base. This required another small loan though. Philip worked six days a week-three days in his office in Oklahoma City and the other three days, he drove the long drive to his office in Sulphur. This was a struggle, and somewhat crazy, but it really helped us at the time.

After we were settled into our new rental home in South Oklahoma City, once again, I felt the Holy Spirit nudging me with a strong calling and desire to form a rosary cenacle for mothers. During the time I was praying about whether to start a group, I began having some sleepless nights. I began having horrible dreams about the devil coming after me. In each dream, his goal was to kill me!

Somehow, I always managed to pray in my sleep and when I did I would wake up. After a few times of this, I began to feel even more strongly about starting the cenacle. A couple of times, I also experienced the smell of roses when I stood near our statue of the Blessed Mother. These unusual experiences brought me to the final decision to begin a women's prayer group I named Mother's Devoted Rosary Group. I felt strongly it was what the Blessed Mother wanted. My passion for this prayer group and my calling were very strong. This time, I put an advertisement in three different church bulletins hoping to get a good group of dedicated mothers. I received a response, but again it was not as many as I would have liked. However, I did get responses from women from the different parishes. Mothers with their children began to meet weekly in my home.

There were a couple of times I worked straightening my house and preparing for the cenacle, but no one showed up, so I would pray the rosary alone. Remember, those were the days before cell phones, so it was a little harder to communicate. This was just part of being a leader. If you feel strongly about something, you have to stay dedicated and be persistent. I always felt we were pleasing to God, even if at times there were only two of us. Christ said, "Where two or three are gathered together in my name, I am there in their midst."

Eventually, our group grew to be about a dozen consistent members and their children. After almost thirty years, we still meet once a month in my home. We still offer our rosary for the priests. We also pray a Litany, Divine Mercy Chaplet, and have time for prayer intentions and sharing. We conclude with consecration prayers to the Sacred Heart of Jesus and the Immaculate Heart of Mary. We love each other, support each other, and pray for each other. I have seen a big strengthening of faith in each member over the years. I have witnessed many incredible answers to prayers. Our children were also able to make some beautiful, lifelong friendships with each other. God has really blessed us all! We have all experienced God's grace from our prayers together. The rosary group has truly been one of the greatest blessings in my life! It is comforting to know that with all the changes going on in our lives, God provided a prayer life and it remained somewhat consistent.

Valley of Tears

In January 1992, it appeared things were going well for our family. Philip's practice was growing with patients. The Mother's Devoted Rosary Group was starting to really bond with good support and friendships, which would eventually become a great blessing for me in the cross I was about to carry. During this busy and hopeful time in our lives, we started noticing Danielle had begun showing unusual physical symptoms.

On her fourth birthday, my mother commented on how very pale she looked in her pink dress. Danielle, being half Mexican, had always had a dark complexion. She also complained of headaches and a sore throat. Bruises began appearing on her arms and legs along with red spots called petechiae. One day while coming home from preschool, I noticed her gums were bleeding. I had asked her if she had fallen or bumped into something. She told me nothing had happened, which I found to be very odd. The final symptom, a pain in her leg, gave us the most concern. By the next day, she began to limp. All of these symptoms came on suddenly.

Philip knew something very serious was wrong. He believed Danielle probably had leukemia or thalassemia minor, a less serious problem. He was hoping it was the latter, but was almost certain it was leukemia. I made an appointment with our family doctor to confirm what it was and took her myself. Even though we thought Danielle's diagnosis could be serious, we decided Philip should go to his office in Sulphur. Looking back on it, we both wish he would have been there.

On 28 January 1992, when I took Danielle to the doctor, I was nervous but calm. Danielle had no idea that she might have a serious problem. The doctor looked at Danielle quickly and stated she needed a blood test. He did not tell me why a blood test was needed or what he suspected was her problem. He sent me over to one of the local city hospitals. On the way to the hospital, I made the mistake of telling four-year-old Danielle she needed a blood test. I explained the procedure and told her it would only hurt a little, but it was very necessary and something had to be done. She began to get very upset! When we arrived at the hospital, she was throwing such a fit that I could not get her out of the car! I was not able to take a screaming, kicking child into the hospital. I saw it as an impossible task. I was stressed and scared myself over the whole ordeal and I wasn't in the mood to be alone in case the worst diagnosis would be given. Keep in mind, cell phones were not around at this time, so I was completely on my own with her.

I decided to take Danielle back home and wait for Philip to come home. It was late in the evening when he arrived home, so we decided to take Danielle to the emergency room at Children's Hospital in Oklahoma City. We took a candy bar for Danielle because we thought it would help her to pass time in the waiting room. My parents watched our other two girls at their home. This night turned out to be the beginning of a long nightmare.

After a long night in the waiting room, Danielle's name was finally called. Danielle was very frightened, but so far she was cooperating. The doctor on duty examined Danielle and stated she could possibly have leukemia. She ordered a blood test to verify. Philip and I remained in the examination room with Danielle while we waited for the nurses to come and draw her blood. She began to cry and grow more frightened. Finally, two nurses entered the room wearing gloves. They both were holding their hands up as if they were prepared for surgery. When they saw Danielle was terrified and screaming, they knew they needed added assistance. A few more nurses came in to help hold her down. The nurses seemed very cold and business-like in their work. I think this made things even worse. They wrapped Danielle tight in a sheet with only her arm able to be free.

Thankfully, they drew her blood in the first try. We were then sent back into another room to wait for the dreaded results. I remember Philip and me looking at each other and we both began to cry. We were trying to hold and comfort each other and Danielle at the same time. Danielle kept crying and saying she wanted to go home. We did not tell her there was a chance she might have to stay in the hospital.

Finally, our name was called. By this time, it was already midnight. The day seemed so long. The doctor who had examined Danielle brought us into a room and asked us to be seated. She told us from the blood test it looked like Danielle had leukemia, but it would have to be confirmed with further tests. We both stayed calm and fought back our tears. She told us Danielle's blood counts were very low and she would need blood transfusions. All of the tests and blood transfusions would require a stay in the hospital, but she had no idea of how long Danielle would have to stay hospitalized. When the doctor left, we stayed calm and cried quietly, trying our best to be strong so as to not frighten Danielle more. We also had to find a phone and call our families to let them know the tragic news.

We had to wait for a hospital transporter to take us to Danielle's room. Danielle was settling down. In fact, she found it exciting when we told her she will have to spend the night at a hospital. When we entered the room, she was actually excited, looking at the bed and bathtub with a big smile on her face. She imagined this would be like staying at a hotel. I wanted to cry so much but I remained as strong as I could for her sake. She was so innocent to the horror coming for her and for us all.

We had to make a decision about what to do with our other two girls, so it was decided for Philip to go home to be with them. We did not want to be a burden to my parents by leaving our kids with them overnight. They had to cope with this news also. Philip hugged and kissed me goodbye as we both cried quietly. Again, I really wish he could have stayed.

After Philip left, I put Danielle to bed by saying our prayers and singing religious songs. She was very tired, so she fell asleep very quickly. It was time for me to go to bed, but there was no bed for me in the room. I didn't realize all I had to do was ask the nurse for a chair-bed. I took my coat and spread it out on the cold hospital floor next to Danielle's bed and laid down. I cried myself to sleep that night and many nights thereafter. I really regret our decision for me to stay with Danielle by myself. I have never felt so scared and lonely in all my life. It was hard for me to grasp how this could be happening. Danielle had always been such a healthy little girl. It was impossible to think clearly. The whole ordeal seemed beyond my human comprehension. I stormed heaven, calling on Jesus, Mary, and the Angels many times to give me comfort. I prayed a lot to the Holy Spirit to give me peace and the strength to endure all the pain.

It was that week of my life, that week of absorbing a shocking tragedy, I felt the presence of God stronger than any other time in my life. When I was alone with Danielle in the hospital at night, it always seemed as if there was someone next to us comforting us. I believe there were angels surrounding us in our hospital room. On one occasion, I remember holding my hand out and asking Jesus to hold it, telling Him how scared I was. Some would say I had a wild imagination, but I felt Jesus very lightly holding my hand and stroking my hair. This immediately gave me peace and I was able to sleep.

Every time I felt myself crying and very upset, I asked the Holy Spirit to give me peace and my crying ceased. I was covered with a blanket of peace. God has never left me alone with my crosses. He has always been there with me. I just have to ask for His help and lay all my problems in His hands, believing with complete trust and faith He will take care of me and my family. Over the years, I have learned the more I let go and trust, then the more my prayers are likely to be answered.

When Danielle and I awoke the next day, 28 January 1992, we were given the biggest cross of our lives and we accepted it with loving trust. Philip did not get to be there with us because he already had patients scheduled and there was no way to contact them to reschedule their appointments. It was I who had to fight the battle alone that day. I don't know why I always found myself alone in those difficult situations when I felt like I needed support the most. This trial in my life reminds me of the 'Hail Holy Queen' prayer recited following the Holy Rosary. In this prayer are the words, 'To thee do we cry mourning and weeping in this valley of tears'. I felt I was living in that valley. It also calls to mind when Jesus was going through his passion, Joseph was not there to comfort Mary. Believe me, all of Heaven was called on that day and many days thereafter. We could not have survived without the strength from God, our Catholic faith, and our entire community of friends and family. Everyone's love and prayers were poured out upon us, holding us tightly and giving us extra strength.

During that sorrowful morning, Danielle and I were taken downstairs to the hematology-oncology clinic at Children's Hospital. Danielle was given a sedative to help prepare her for the procedure she was about ready to have, but it was not effective. She was wide awake and very aware of everything around her. Later, we were to find out this particular medication had the ability to cause her temporary depression. When Danielle's name was called, we were taken into a room where the doctor would perform a painful bone marrow test to determine her exact diagnosis. She was told to lay on her stomach and be as still as possible.

Thankfully, I was able to remain in the room with her. She was scared and crying very hard. A couple of nurses were brought in to help hold her down. She was fighting with great strength! From the size of the needle, I could tell she had a very good reason to be frightened. It was very long and looked to be twice to three times the size of the diameter of an air pump needle. In order to produce enough force to puncture the hip bone, the doctor had to put all his weight over the needle. As the doctor spent about ten minutes drawing out about a dozen vials of bone marrow, it was obvious Danielle was in severe pain. It was horrible!

I kept telling myself I had to keep my composure for Danielle's sake, but my tears were unstoppable. I kept talking to Danielle and trying to comfort her the best I could or knew how. I was praying for her the entire time. I only wish it could have taken the pain away! Finally, the bone marrow test and the immense pain was over, though she remained very sore for days.

After the procedure came the dreaded results. I was happy and relieved when Philip showed up just as the doctor was explaining things to me. He told us Danielle had been diagnosed with acute lymphocytic leukemia. This type of leukemia had an eighty percent survival rate for children between the ages of two and ten years old. Danielle was four and a half. This gave us a lot of hope. He told us he expected Danielle to achieve remission in the next four weeks.

Then, she would begin two and one half years of weekly chemotherapy. The first six months of the chemotherapy would include hospital stays every other week. Outpatient chemotherapy would be given in the weeks she was not hospitalized. Her hospital stays were to be two or three nights at a time. It would be very daunting and stressful.

We asked the doctor what would happen if Danielle relapsed. He told us if she relapsed her chances would be reversed. She would have only a twenty percent chance of survival and her chemotherapy would be started over with a new two and one half year course. Again, Philip and I were very strong and kept our composure. When the doctor left the room, we held each other and cried. We talked about how God would help us. We knew we just had to have a lot of faith. I just wanted someone to pinch me and wake me up from this horrible nightmare. At times, I thought back to when I dedicated Danielle and her life to God before she was born. I prayed for the ability to accept whatever may happen to her. I also prayed if it be God's will, He would allow her to be healed. Our prayers were continuous throughout her illness.

Danielle had to keep an IV in her arm during her whole stay in the hospital. She also had to have her finger stuck with a needle for blood counts every day. Many times, the nurse would use a painful lance. When Danielle would see the lance, she always became very scared. Eventually, I bought Danielle her very own finger prick machine which she found to be less painful, but some stubborn nurses would refuse to use it. Before we left the hospital, she had a band aid on almost every finger. She always hated having her bandages removed. She also learned to detest the smell of rubbing alcohol, since she associated it with pain. The first week she was diagnosed, her hips and legs were in so much pain. I had to massage them frequently. She was so sore and weak I had to carry her to the bathroom, while pulling her IV pole. This was a challenge since she weighed about forty-two pounds. Unfortunately, that first hospital stay we had the worst moving pole in the hospital! Little did I know we could have just asked for a different one. We would learn a lot over the next couple of years of hospital stays.

On the second full day of Danielle's initial hospital stay, she had more tests to endure, such as, X-rays, bone scans, ultrasound, and finally, a spinal tap. This time, Philip was there to help me since the first bone marrow test was such a horrible experience. I was not quite ready to watch Danielle endure more suffering.

The next major test to be done was a spinal tap. A syringe would be injected into her spine to take spinal fluid out. By this time, it was very difficult to get Danielle to cooperate with anything. Philip had to carry her out kicking and screaming. I stayed in her hospital room and cried. I held my rosary and tried to pray the best I could through all my tears. A mother of another leukemia patient saw me so distraught and came into my room to help comfort me. I felt it must have been Jesus who inspired this woman to talk with me and comfort me. She was very kind and caring. It was very helpful to have someone near me who had already been through the same kind of real-life nightmare I was experiencing.

Danielle had to endure spinal taps every six weeks. I was not there for her first, but I was right next to her for all the remaining ones. During these awful spinal taps, Danielle was always wide awake and alert. She was given a local anesthetic, but Danielle said she could always feel it. She had to lay on her side, curled up in a fetal position. The doctor would then insert a long needle into her spinal cord. Spinal fluid was drawn out and then chemotherapy was administered back into her spine. Danielle never showed leukemia cells in her spinal fluid, thank God, but the chemotherapy was preventive.

I will never forget one of Danielle's worst spinal tap experiences. She always had to be held tightly to keep her from moving. Even though she knew it was very important for her to remain still, she always put up a tremendous fight. This time the usual nurse who held Danielle was not available. A different nurse was doing the holding, and she was having a very difficult time. Therefore, the doctor was having a very hard time finding the spinal cord with her needle. She had already poked Danielle several times unsuccessfully. Danielle was screaming and crying loudly. Then to make matters worse, she needed to use the bathroom. I kept telling her it would be over soon. If she could only wait a little longer. There were a couple of nursing students standing there watching, since it was a teaching hospital, and my father, John, was there also to support me. I know this was terribly hard for him. After much effort, another male doctor was called in to help hold Danielle.

Danielle continued to complain of needing to go to the bathroom. She could hold it no longer. She began wetting herself all over the table. Again, the nursing students were standing there watching. I felt so sorry for her. My heart was breaking. She was not only enduring every suffering of pain, but also total humiliation! I know wetting her pants in front of a crowd was an ultimate embarrassment for her. Normally, she had excellent bladder control. She was just asked to do the impossible! Tears were streaming down my face as I tried to comfort her. Even though I had prayed for Danielle with all my heart, it seemed to be to no avail! Relief was just not there. The only thing I could think of is she was called to suffer for someone special that day and there was no prayer that could take away her pain.

I did feel the prayers always gave her strength to endure. I heard another mother once say Jesus comforts suffering children through their mothers. So, it's actually a beautiful grace to be a parent and allow Jesus to comfort our children through us.

Danielle remained in the hospital for ten days that first stay. During that time, she became very depressed. Later, we learned massive doses of the steroid Prednisone had terrible effect on her. Her little, happy life no longer seemed happy. She rarely said a word, other than 'yes' or 'no'. Hardly anyone could make her smile. A clown, named 'La-La', came to visit to try and cheer her up. The clown spent a long and hard time trying to get Danielle to laugh to no avail. Not only would she not smile, she would not even show any facial expressions at all! It hurt so much to see this once jolly, little girl so unhappy. It was another painful suffering we endured.

Another pleasant visitor during her first hospital stay was Fr Mike Chapman. He was a friend of the family. He came to administer to Danielle the Sacrament of the Sick. He then asked me how well Danielle understood the concept of Jesus in the Eucharist. I told him, "Very well." I had taught Danielle quite a bit about the Eucharist and I knew she really believed it was Jesus' truly present Body, Blood, Soul and Divinity.

Fr Chapman asked Danielle if there was a difference between the hosts in the entrance of the church and the hosts people took at Communion. Danielle knew the answer and said, "Yes, the hosts in the front of the church are bread, but the hosts people get at Communion are Jesus." I think Father was surprised by her confident and definite response. He said since Danielle's life was in danger with leukemia, not yet in remission, he would allow her the special privilege of her first Holy Communion at the age of four. This was one time in the hospital that brought Danielle much joy and peace. She was so happy and thrilled to receive Jesus in the Holy Eucharist. The clown could not make Danielle smile, but Jesus did! Ironically, Fr Chapman was the same priest who gave me my first Holy Communion at St. James Church when I was seven years old.

On another occasion, Fr George Pupius, the pastor of our parish, came and brought Danielle Holy Communion. After receiving the Eucharist, she told me she didn't care for the taste of the host, but she was still always very eager to receive it. She truly believed it was Jesus she was receiving. I had explained to Danielle how powerful her prayers were in those first few moments right after receiving Communion, and that Jesus was united with her in a powerful way.

Strength to Endure

After ten long days of torturous hospital treatment, we were more than ready to return home. Finally, we got the doctor's orders that Danielle could go home. However, she was to be put on large amounts of steroids for the next four months. We were told it was very likely she would lose all her long, curly hair and gain a lot of weight from the medications. We were dreading this experience, but at least we got to go home.

Danielle was very happy to be home with her family and her new, red bunk bed she had missed. We had just bought the bunk bed days before she started her hospital stay. As expected, the massive doses of steroids made her hungry and eat excessively. They caused her cheeks and stomach to swell a great deal. She gained a lot of weight in a short period of time.

Usually, Danielle was very sweet, patient, and kind. But it seemed now so many things irritated her, especially her sisters crying. Her temperament changed drastically. She would get really angry and upset if I did not give her something to eat right away. This was not like her at all. She would not move from the couch. She had no energy and she would become very agitated when her sisters would sit next to her. This was very hard on them. They did not understand what was happening to their loving big sister who was their best friend. I cried many times over these things that were completely out of my control. I was sad, but never became depressed. These times were very hard for all of us. None of us received counseling other than the strength and grace we were given through all the prayers and the Sacraments of the Church.

Since we were told Danielle would lose all of her hair, I had it cut short. She had long, curly ringlets and I couldn't bear the thought of her hair coming out by the handfuls. Danielle looked so different with all the changes going on. Her hair was short and she had gained so much weight in such a short time. Her cheeks were very puffy. Her personality seemed to have totally changed as well. It was as though we were in the Twilight Zone. We all wanted so badly to return to the way things were. We had no idea how this devil of leukemia would affect Danielle and our lives in so many different areas. All we wanted was our old Danielle back and our lives to be normal.

Amazingly, Danielle did not lose any of her hair! We found great comfort in this simple, small gift of hair. When she was first diagnosed, I asked God for a sign she would be completely healed. The requested sign was for Danielle to keep all of her hair through the chemotherapy treatments. It gave us hope that all would eventually be well.

Faith, Hope, and Love

The day arrived for the bone marrow test that would tell us if she had achieved remission. If she had, she would be taken off the horrible steroids and would begin her two and a half year chemotherapy treatment plan. This bone marrow test did not take nearly as long as the first, but it was still very uncomfortable and painful. The test came back negative. As expected, Danielle had achieved remission only four weeks after being diagnosed. We were very thankful to God. We felt and hoped this was a beginning to the answer of our prayers.

Heaven was stormed with prayers of petition and Thanksgiving. For her part, Danielle also prayed and did other acts of faith for healing. She drank healing holy waters from different locations, such as healing water from the fountain at Lourdes, France. She even ate a blessed rose petal that was promised to cure her. She did these very willingly because she trusted and she believed in God's healing power. We had people giving us blessed things from everywhere. An incredible amount of people were praying for her healing.

On one occasion, I took Danielle to see a famous healing priest, Fr Ralph Diorio, who happened to be in

Oklahoma City. Fr Diorio stood on the stage and called out different types of ailments and sometimes would describe a specific person and tell them they were healed. When he said those with leukemia or people with infection in their blood would feel their blood boil if they were experiencing a healing, Danielle complained of being very hot. She had to remove her jacket and I had to fan her. Also, she was the first one he anointed when he stepped down from the stage, we felt she had been healed. To this day, I feel she was receiving gifts and healing from the Holy Spirit, but the physical healing was only temporary. What the Spirit gave her was the strength to endure. Philip and I had one hundred percent faith Danielle had been healed. Sometimes, people would ask me, "What if she relapses?"

I would tell them, "I do not think about it," because I believed she was healed. Just to settle their mind, though, I would tell them, "if she did relapse, it would not destroy my faith." I explained to them, I knew the Holy Spirit would give me the strength to handle my cross and the love to accept it.

The Holy Spirit did give us great strength and a peace to handle everything ahead of us in response to all the prayers being offered for Danielle and our family. Since we had no medical insurance when she was diagnosed, some very good friends started a medical fund for Danielle.

Today, we can see why God had intended it to be that way. So many people learned of Danielle through 'The Danielle Martinez Fund'. Also, later on in her illness, a story was written about her and the Fund in *The Sooner Catholic*, the local diocesan newspaper. The paper was sent throughout the diocese and throughout the country to all those who used to live in the diocese. It seemed many fell in love with her and wanted to pray for her recovery and healing. Gifts to the fund and prayer cards were coming in from all over. If we had been insured at the time of Danielle's diagnosis, the fund would not have been established and there would not have been nearly as many people praying. It was also humbling for us to depend on others for their help in our situation. God intended it to be this way.

Sometimes, when we look at the world through our own eyes, everything can seem so messed up, but when we try to view it with God's eyes, it all makes perfect sense. It's easy to get upset and wonder why our prayers are not being answered. Our prayers are always being heard, but as a loving Father, He does not always give us everything we want. He gives us what we need. Only He knows what is best for us in our situations in life. We must always trust in Him with a childlike trust. Many times, if our prayers were answered in the way we ask for them, we would miss out on a lot of good learning experiences and spiritual growth. St. Catherine of Sienna said it best when she said, "There are more tears shed by prayers answered the way we would want them than those that are not."

We realized prayer was Danielle's main source of strength, but she also received additional help from a child psychologist from Children's Hospital named Anne. A few months after Danielle was diagnosed, she grew tired of all the shots, finger sticks, spinal taps and IVs. Getting her to her weekly appointments became a real challenge. Spiritually, I feel Danielle was well beyond her years, but mentally, she was still just a small child. Sometimes, she would put up such a fight. We had to carry her out to the car literally kicking and screaming. We had to struggle to put her in the car and lock the door, hoping she wouldn't try to jump out as the car was moving. Philip and I had to alternate taking her to her appointments. I cried often as we put her in the car, watching her scream with terror as she banged her hands on the windows of the car.

One day, as Philip was driving down the street, she did manage to open the car door, but Philip stopped the car in time and she was not hurt. On the days Philip took her, I would go back into the house and cry. This was so incredibly hard for all of us. I felt Danielle's psychologist helped her a lot with this. Anne was very patient and loving with Danielle. Eventually, Danielle began to accept the treatments, but still did not like them. As she grew older, the leg shots became easier for her and she did not even want me to be in the room with her! She actually enjoyed spending time talking to some of the nurses whom she grew to love.

Growing in Faith

Danielle's treatment plan was vigorous and very time-consuming. One week, we would go to the clinic for a finger stick for blood counts and a shot of chemotherapy in the leg. The clinic visits were never short. The next week, we would spend a few nights in the hospital with chemotherapy given through an IV. Dispersed throughout were the spinal taps and bone marrow tests to see if her treatment was working. It started to become very monotonous. Danielle was beginning to hate Tuesdays, which was her clinic day. All our many hours of waiting helped teach us patience.

Offering up suffering to help other souls is something Danielle learned about. She grew a great deal in wisdom for being such a young child. She understood this well and had many opportunities to practice. Sometimes, before a shot or one of her spinal taps, I would remind her to offer her suffering to help a soul in Purgatory or for someone who needed conversion. Sometimes she would say, "I know, I remember." I know this helped her endure her pain and suffering since she knew it would help someone else. Once, she offered her spinal tap for her little cousin who was diagnosed with a physical problem. She asked Jesus that by her suffering her cousin would be healed and he was! She was very loving and had a great desire to help others. As stated earlier, Danielle was a very spiritual little girl and was blessed with wisdom beyond her years.

We taught Danielle her faith, but she also experienced a very special closeness to God in many different ways. On one instance, when she was four years old, she awoke one morning in a very excited and joyful state. She came running into the room and told me she had a beautiful dream about angels singing. She said she and her daddy were standing outside looking up into the clouds and they saw many angels singing in beautiful voices. They were nothing like anything she had ever heard before. She was smiling and rambled on and on about how beautifully they sang. As I reflect on this, I feel this was a revelation of her death that would take place only a couple of years later. For you see, when she died, she was all alone with her daddy, and I have no doubt she heard beautiful angels singing.

On another similar occasion, when Danielle was about five, she awoke from another joyful and beautiful dream. Again, she showed the same enthusiasm and excitement she portrayed before, when she dreamed of the angels singing.

She said she had a dream about Mary holding baby Jesus. Mary was very beautiful with long, dark hair. She was wearing a pink dress. In her arms was the Child Jesus dressed in green. Mary was standing over a bush or tree. I asked Danielle if Mary said anything, and she said, "No, she only looked at me and smiled." Danielle was glowing with joy all morning! I felt the Blessed Mother and the Infant Jesus did visit her in her sleep, letting her know how happy they were with her and assuring her of their love. What a beautiful consolation for Danielle from all of her many tears!

One day, when Danielle was in kindergarten at Sacred Heart School, she came home excited, similar to the ways she awoke from her beautiful dreams. She told me while she was attending school mass, she saw the statue of the Sacred Heart of Jesus look at her and smile. I asked her if she saw the statue turn its head, trying to see if this was imagination and she would play along. She said, "No, He just looked at me and smiled." She was so happy! Who knows if this happened or if she imagined it? It does not matter. What matters is that Jesus let her feel His love and His approval of her little life of love and suffering.

Danielle showed she loved Jesus and wanted to please Him. On many occasions, I found her praying alone without anyone telling her to do so. When she was four, I would often find her in her bedroom praying a chaplet to her favorite saint, St. Therese, the Little Flower. This chaplet contains twenty-four Glory Be's. Between each prayer it is said, "St. Therese of the Child Jesus, pray for us." This was a lengthy prayer which took a lot of concentration to hold a small child's attention, but it was something she loved doing.

At other times, when Danielle was five, she would often be reciting the rosary on her own. On one particular occasion, she was outside in front of our house kneeling before our yard statue of the Blessed Virgin Mary. She was busy reciting the rosary by herself. Her sisters were off playing and she had left them to go pray. We were very happy to see her show such great faith and love for God!

Sometimes, I found Danielle lying on her bed with a small icon of Mary and the Infant Jesus her grandmother gave her. Sometimes, when Danielle was in pain, she would take the icon off her wall above her bed and look at it with love and many times, the pain would subside.

She loved holy pictures and statues. They helped remind her of the presence of God and His saints. The thought of them helped a great deal when she was in pain or suffering in other ways. In one of the treatment rooms at the hospital clinic, there was a picture of Jesus with the little children sitting on his lap. This was her favorite treatment room because she liked to focus on that picture before she got her shot.

There were other things that helped Danielle to focus on the spiritual world. One was a small blessed wooden angel my mother gave to her. Sometimes, she brought this angel with her to the clinic when she knew she would be having a painful procedure. The wooden angel was to remind Danielle that her own guardian angel was always with her, praying for her and giving comfort. Another consolation was a crucifix containing a relic of the true cross of Christ. These relics are obtained through the Vatican for people in special situations. The relic comes with a certificate of authenticity. We were only able to obtain it with the help of a special priest. She held it, kissed it, and blessed herself with it often. We also used the relic and asked God to bless us and give us strength.

Danielle always seemed to have heavenly thoughts. She expressed this in her drawings of religious pictures in her free time at home and at school. Once, when Danielle was four, she drew a picture with a blue marker of the twelve apostles. Hovering above their heads, she drew the tongues of fire. Up in the clouds, she drew a circle with a sign on it. When I questioned her about what it was, she told me it was Jesus in Holy Communion. When she showed me this picture and explained it to me, I was amazed at the spiritual maturity of such a small child. It made me feel really good to know she understood and loved her Catholic faith and had been learning it well. I feel only a picture inspired by the Holy Spirit could be so beautiful. Sadly, I cannot find this picture today. I wish we had kept it.

She drew many pictures of Jesus hanging on the cross with nails in His hands and feet. She also drew pictures of Jesus with Mary. I wondered what her kindergarten teacher thought since she drew so many religious pictures. As Danielle grew older and learned more about different saints, she liked drawing pictures of them. She developed devotions with many of the saints, such as St. Peregrine, the patron of cancer victims, St. Therese of the Child Jesus, to whom she learned to offer her sufferings, and St. Blaze, the patron saint of throats, because she felt they could help her with her illness. On many occasions, Danielle suffered from a burning sensation in her throat caused by the chemotherapy and would ask St. Blaze for his prayers. My mother gave her a small statue of St. Therese she would pack in her bag for her hospital stays. She would keep it on the table next to her hospital bed during her overnight stays.

Danielle also enjoyed learning about the lives of many saints from different story books and videos we had. I feel it is important for children to learn about the saints' lives, so that they can have good heroic role models to follow. Saints can be very inspirational as we journey in our faith.

Danielle was also a good evangelizer for being so young. She liked to draw with sidewalk chalk on our driveway. Many of her drawings were religious in nature. One day, Danielle drew a picture of an open book the size of the driveway and in it she wrote, "I love Jesus and Mary and God and Joseph." Anyone who drove by could see this. It was a witness of her faith.

Other occasions where she showed spiritual leadership were at night. Almost every night, in order for the girls to fall asleep, Philip would get in Danielle's bed and I would get in Dominique and Gabrielle's bed. About when Philip would get comfortable and almost fall asleep, he would get a knock on the top of his head. Danielle would say, "Daddy, we forgot to say our prayers." She would be persistent until he led us in prayer. Once I asked her if she remembered to pray more than just her night prayers, and she told me, "Yes, sometimes, I pray while I'm playing."

A Gift From God

Two months after Danielle was diagnosed with leukemia, I found myself pregnant with our fourth child. Danielle was still going through her hospital protocol and we were still uninsured. We knew I would probably have premature labor as I did with the other children. Somehow, this just did not seem like the perfect timing, but evidently God felt it was. Again, many people ridiculed us for the pregnancy. Some people could not understand why we would let this happen. What they really did not comprehend was why we let God control our lives. Most people criticized or judged out of ignorance. I understood their concerns, but we had to, once again, surrender ourselves to Jesus and trust in His plans. I regretfully say, at the beginning of the pregnancy, I was so sad and worried about being pregnant again that I had to confess this sin in Confession. I hope in the future, I will accept all my crosses with a kiss and with love. God is always in control and He truly knows what is best for our lives.

Once the initial shock was over, I began getting excited about my sweet baby's arrival. I prayed a lot for this pregnancy, especially for the intercession of St. Gerard, the Patron Saint of Mothers. Also, to Our Lady of Guadalupe, the Patroness of the Unborn. I prayed several novenas and put my trust in God that He would bring this baby safely into the world.

I consecrated this child to the Sacred Heart of Jesus and to Our Lady of Guadalupe, just as I had consecrated my other children before they were born. I also asked for a special pregnant mother's blessing from Fr George Pupius. As he touched my forehead to bless me, I felt as though I was going to come off the ground. My feet felt light and almost elevated. The presence of the Holy Spirit was very strong and similar to the feeling I had in the dream of Jesus blessing me when I was pregnant with Danielle.

Philip still had his practice in Sulphur, but I needed him closer to home to help me with Danielle's treatment program, Dominique and Gabrielle, and the preparation for the new baby. He was gone from home a lot and I felt overwhelmed. I had to keep up with the girls and the housework. Occasionally, I would even mow our lawn while late in my pregnancy. I kept praying he would sell his practice in Sulphur or close it. However, the practice was bringing us added income and Philip did not want to give it up. It did not take long for my prayers to get answered. The building the office was operating out of was sold and the new owner needed the entire space. Without this office, Philip was able to arrange his schedule at his Oklahoma City office, so he could spend more time with us and at the clinic with Danielle.

Even with Philip's help, the overnight hospital stays for Danielle were definitely not easy. They became more burdensome as I grew in my pregnancy. I spent many nights sleeping in a hard, uncomfortable hospital chair-bed. As my pregnancy progressed, it got more and more uncomfortable. Mentally, it bothered me as well, because I knew my other little girls were at home longing for their mother.

Then, in September 1992, we were relieved to find out Danielle's hospital stays for chemotherapy were over! She continued weekly chemotherapy, but it was given on an outpatient basis. This could not have happened at a better time because, as soon as the therapy ended, the baby began to threaten to come prematurely. I was put on medication and total bed rest once again. When I was twenty-nine weeks pregnant, I ended up at the hospital because of premature labor. After my contractions were under control, I was sent home and told to take my medication and I was to do nothing. Though this was a suffering, it gave me a wonderful opportunity to pray more and to read religious books, ordinarily, I would not have ever had time to read. God planned it this way because He knew it was an opportunity to grow closer to Him and a time to prepare myself for the care of a new, loving little soul in our lives. It became my spiritual retreat.

During this time, there was a traveling picture of Our Lady of Guadalupe that was making its way around in our parish. We were able to keep this picture in our home during my bed rest. I began to pray for her intercession for the safety of my delivery and I consecrated my baby's soul to Our Lady of Guadalupe.

On 18 November 1992, our first little boy arrived. He was three weeks premature, but was strong and very healthy. We named him Nathanael Luke, which means 'gift from God'. God definitely knows when to plan children because he was just what we all needed, especially Danielle.

He gave us all a gift of joy as we struggled in suffering throughout the last two years of Danielle's life. Since I had consecrated Nathanael to Our Lady of Guadalupe, we had him baptized on 12 December, the Feast of Our Lady of Guadalupe and gave him the name Guadalupe for a Baptismal name. At Confirmation, he took the name Juan Diego. On a side note, ironically, as an adult, Nathanael studied abroad in Mexico. He fell in love with a young woman there, got married in the Catholic Church, and moved to Puebla, Mexico, which is not far from Mexico City where Mary appeared to Juan Diego. Amazingly, God knew before he was even born where he would be someday and had a wonderful plan for his life!

Nathanael's three sisters smothered him with love and attention, but it was Danielle who I felt needed this little joy the most. Nathanael made her laugh when no one else was able. She always loved to watch him and be close to him. Everything he did brought a smile to her face. Nathanael was Danielle's sunshine in her rain storm. There is no way to explain the great love she had for her baby brother and two little sisters. I am sure she prays for them constantly, even now.

Nathanael was a very affectionate little boy. Frequently, he told all of us he loved us. He loved to give kisses and hugs to everyone. I'm sure the girls' love and affection toward him had a lot to do with his loving ways. In many ways, Nathanael resembled Danielle. They both were very well-behaved, loved others and had spiritual awareness beyond their years. It had already become obvious to us, Nathanael had tremendous love for Jesus and His Blessed Mother. I think he learned this love from me, but also from his sisters. They enjoyed teaching him everything they knew. When he was only two years old, he knew how to genuflect and make the sign of the cross.

I'm sure Danielle continues to help all her siblings to grow in their faith and her greatest desire is to help them reach eternal life. Faith is such a constant learning and growing process.

Others Getting to Know Danielle

In 1993, Danielle attended all-day kindergarten at Sacred Heart Catholic School. She was very intelligent and an excellent reader. At first, she thought she would learn a lot going to school, but because it was easy, she became bored with repetitive work. She began to really miss her brother and sisters. Many times, she would complain about going to school. Danielle was never a morning person and waking up early was always hard. Then it became twice as hard because she was advanced and found school boring. Added to these difficulties was the fact she would feel sick to her stomach because of the chemotherapy. Sometimes, when she felt really bad, she would lay down on a carpet on the classroom floor. Her sweet teacher would give her crackers and 7-Up to help get her get through the day.

During her kindergarten year at school, she met a little girl who really got on her nerves. Danielle would come home from school and tell me most everything that had happened in her day. One thing she was always bothered about was the lies and stories this girl told. This little girl also copied from Danielle's work and was sometimes mean to other children in her class. The behavior of this classmate really bothered Danielle, but she always continued to be nice to her. My advice was to be very nice to the little girl and pray for her. At times, the other girls in the class would not allow this girl to play with them. So out of kindness, Danielle would sacrifice playing with her friends and play with this girl because she felt sorry for the girl and did not like seeing her alone.

Later in the semester, when I picked up Danielle's report card, I told the teacher about the little girl who seemed to bother and annoy Danielle. The teacher said she was very surprised to hear there was a problem. She had always thought the girl and Danielle were best friends. Danielle was always so loving and kind to everyone. For example, Danielle told me if she saw someone alone on the playground, she would go up to them and ask them to play. I know it was the love of Jesus in her heart that brought out her compassion for others.

Another problem arose that school year. There was a little boy in the first grade class who used to run from her on the playground because she had leukemia. He said he was afraid he might catch it. When Danielle first told me this, it upset me because I thought it would hurt her feelings, but then when she started laughing about it; I could see it did not bother her at all! She knew he was ignorant about leukemia and she found it humorous that he was afraid. Danielle always showed a great sense of humor.

Though Danielle had a severe illness, she never let it stop her from enjoying life. She always had a determination about her. While at Sacred Heart School, Danielle joined the school's soccer team and managed to play very well. She enjoyed soccer so much and never lacked athletic talent. She always hustled and tried hard, giving it her all even at practices. She was very competitive. Also, in the fall, she began to take weekly piano lessons. I never had to make her practice because she loved it so much. We discovered she really had a good ear for music. Perhaps, she took after her great grandmother who taught piano and organ for more than forty years. Her grandmother also played piano, organ, and classical guitar. Several of our kids have excelled in musical instruments and one in singing and musical theater. Danielle showed her talent in two piano recitals in which she had to memorize a few musical pieces. She played them very well. It became obvious she had musical talent. She was in a piano guild where her playing abilities were judged and she was given a report card. She made a perfect score!

Sometimes, she would think about a tune and go over to the piano and try to play it by ear. She was very good at this. I found her at the piano often without needing to be asked. She especially loved it when she got a new music piece to learn. She always liked a challenge. I loved hearing her sit at the piano, making up her own songs. She would spend hours playing and singing along with her music. She had such a pretty, little singing voice. We were all so proud of Danielle and her beautiful, discovered talent of music. I told her if she got really good at piano, later, I would allow her to take voice lessons. She was really looking forward to the day she could take those lessons. I'm sure if ever given the chance, she would have loved musical theater. Performing and entertaining was fun and came easy to her. It was hard to believe she had a life-threatening disease because she appeared so normal!

In the spring of Danielle's kindergarten year, she decided she wanted to play soccer again. We got her on a team in an Oklahoma City soccer league. She played for a very competitive co-ed team called the Bears. Because she liked soccer so much, the hard work and all the running did not seem to bother her at all. She had really improved her soccer playing so much that it seemed she was one of the better players on the team. The other parents could not believe she had leukemia. Her practices lasted for one and a half hours and were very tiring, especially after a long day of school.

When the team had to run, she was usually in the front of the pack. This was not because of great speed, it was more because of her determination and desire to try hard. Danielle was very confident in her soccer playing. She felt besides school and piano, this was one physical thing she could really do well. That would explain why she enjoyed it so much. Sometimes, she also liked to dribble the basketball and talked about how she looked forward to playing another sport, as well.

It seemed like she excelled in everything she did. Her personality was laid back and easy going, but very competitive. Being a very good reader, she would love to sit and read a stack of books. Her favorite books were about history. She enjoyed reading the lives of the saints, the presidents of the United States, and about Native Americans. She was very good at geography and identifying the fifty US states. She was good at math, but unless it was difficult and gave her a challenge, she did not like it. Sometimes, her work from school looked sloppy. When I asked her why, she told me it was boring so she did not put a lot of effort into it. Once at the hematology & oncology clinic at Children's Hospital, she was given an IQ test because a student was doing a study on the combination of chemotherapy and how it might affect the brain and thinking. We were never given the results, but were told she did extremely well.

Typically, Danielle would never say anything to hurt someone's feelings on purpose. She was very caring and considerate. I had taught Danielle to do what Jesus would do. If she was ever unsure of something, I told her she could always ask herself, "What would Jesus do?" She followed this rule really well when it came to others. Being kind to everyone has always been a strong motto in our family. I always teach my kids, you don't have to agree with everyone, but you absolutely must be kind to everyone. Loving everyone and finding Christ in the heart of everyone is a must!

Her sisters gave her more of a challenge, as all family members do. They had a tendency to play with or accidentally break her things, which really upset her. She would argue with them, but more often she was the peacemaker between them. When they were trying to learn something new, she would always compliment them and encourage them. They would fight over who would sit next to her because they said she was so nice to them. They could feel her love. She had a lot to do with building their confidence and self-esteem since she always paid such close attention to them and loved them so much.

One of Danielle's favorite things to play with her sisters was with her Barbie dolls. She had a lot of them. When she was diagnosed with leukemia, many people knew she liked

Barbies, and they gave them to her as gifts. Also, before each major procedure, she would get to pick a toy from the toy closet and almost always, she would choose another Barbie. She had quite a collection. Danielle and her sisters would play together for hours at a time with her Barbies. Danielle really had a creative imagination. They could also spend a long time playing with stuffed animals. She was always the leader and loved to organize their playtime. They loved sharing many things together, such as their bedroom, clothes, toys, meals, family prayers, television shows, and time outside, even baths together. They really stuck together like glue. Where you would find one, you would always find the others.

Danielle desired for everyone to be good. In our daily family prayers, she always reminded us to pray for the conversion of sinners and for the souls in Purgatory. She also offered her suffering for them. I truly feel she loved everyone, no matter what their wrongs or differences were. Several times, she stated to me Jesus wants us to love everyone and I think she did her best to follow this. I prayed with Danielle every day and she was always generous in her prayers. She always thought of praying for others before praying for herself. She never prayed for anything unnecessary like useless material goods. She always seemed content with the things she had, and I could tell by her prayers, she was very grateful to God for what she did have, especially her family.

I think Danielle could have been happy in any kind of environment. She could have been happy anywhere, and in any place, as long as she had her faith and her family. She really seemed to appreciate almost everything.

Danielle had a really good conscience of right from wrong. For instance, if there was a television program she felt might be offensive to God, she quickly turned the channel. She was very good at picking up on things that were not good. She did not have to be told something was right or wrong because she could feel it in her heart. A couple of times, when she was attending kindergarten, there were television programs shown to the kids that Danielle felt were inappropriate. She knew if she were at home, I would not let her watch. They were 'bad shows', as she would call them. Generally, these shows were cartoons with New Age messages in them. She told me instead of watching the shows, she would just sit and think about other things and do her best to avoid looking at them. I felt peer pressure would never be much of a problem for her. She had a good conscience and had the ability to make very good decisions on her own. She was blessed with a good moral compass.

Besides being a good child, Danielle had a bright, beautiful and funny personality. When she was little, she was very shy, but as she grew older, she became a little more outgoing. She always had a really funny sense of humor. She was a lot like her daddy in this sense.

He would tease her and she would tease him back. One of their favorite jokes was concerning birds. She knew her daddy had a fear of birds, so every time there were birds nearby or when there were a lot of birds outside, she would make a caw sound like a crow or she would start whistling the tune from the movie, 'The Birds'. Then, she would start laughing hysterically. She enjoyed teasing him and her sisters. She really enjoyed laughing with her little brother,

Nathanael. She was usually happy, laughing and joyful, unless she was enduring the hospital or pain.

Though she was very good, occasionally she did have to be corrected. Sometimes, she threw some pretty good fits when she did not get her way, but generally, we were the only ones to witness this. When she was with others, she acted very well. From a very early age, Danielle was taught to stop and think about what Jesus would do if He were in her situation. She knew and understood what was right and wrong. She loved God and was always wanting to please Him and her family. She was excellent at minding others and having respect for authority.

Danielle stated to us several times she had a desire to be a nun when she grew up. I think she just wanted to do whatever was pleasing to God. She really wanted to live her life for Him. A priest once told us Danielle would not only have been a great nun, as she wanted to be, but she could have been a great mother superior!

Though she said she wanted to be a nun, she was very boy crazy also. She had a crush on several boys from school. Sometimes, she would come home from school and say, "I don't know who I'm going to marry; there's Robert, Taylor, and Chris." She enjoyed being a little girl full of life and love. She loved sports, but was very feminine. She liked Barbies, dolls, playing in makeup, wearing perfume, and dressing up as a princess. She was confident in herself, but she in no way showed to be conceited or vain. She was very happy being a girl.

Other Setbacks

Besides the leukemia, we had to withstand other trials and tribulations with Danielle. Any kind of illness can be very dangerous when a person is receiving heavy chemotherapy. While chemotherapy does a good job of killing off bad blood cells, it also kills good cells at the same time. This can lower the immune system and make a person very susceptible to other infections.

When she was five, she contracted mononucleosis and had to be hospitalized for about ten days. With any kind of contagious illness, she had to be put in isolation. Every day consisted of watching television or playing video games. This may sound fun, but after a while, it becomes very boring. And knowing she could not leave the room made it even worse. It was like solitary confinement. At age six, Danielle contracted chicken pox from her brother, Nathanael. She had to be hospitalized again for about ten days. Thankfully, this was a mild case. However, while in the hospital, she was fortunate to receive the Sacrament of the Sick and Holy Communion. She only received Communion in times of possible danger until she was seven years old, when she started to receive it regularly. During these times, visitors would come to see her, which helped, but I think, *Many people did not understand the seriousness of having these extra setbacks.*

The shingles was another illness Danielle suffered through. One day, we took her for a regular weekly appointment. She was first examined by a student doctor. She was then given her scheduled; heavy dose of chemotherapy called Adriamycin. After receiving this medication, she began complaining about a little red blister on her cheek. I asked the doctor to re-examine her. After the examination, it was determined Danielle probably had shingles. In order to diagnose this illness correctly, a sample of the blister would have to be taken. To avoid exposing the other patients, we were led to a back room. We were told chickenpox can be contracted from shingles. If this truly was shingles, all of the other children who were in the clinic that day would have to receive a chickenpox vaccine. We felt very bad about possibly exposing others, but we were totally unaware of Danielle having the shingles.

After we were taken into the isolation room, we sat waiting for the doctor to come. He was going to scrape the blister on Danielle's face to get a sample for testing. Danielle was becoming very frightened. She was crying and very upset as she sat on my lap not knowing what to expect. I asked for Anne, her psychologist, to be paged. Anne came and tried talking to Danielle.

She suggested I try reading to Danielle to help distract her from the horrible anticipation of the pain that awaited her. I read Danielle her homeschooling history book about saints. Thankfully, this seemed to help calm her down. When the doctor came in to perform the procedure, Danielle was terrified and it was obvious she was not going to hold still. She was just too frightened. The doctor decided Danielle needed a sedative. She was given an injection through her catheter. While we were waiting for the drug to take effect, my father came to help comfort us. I explained to him if she did have shingles, she would be admitted into the hospital and stay until the shingles scabbed over.

I continued reading to Danielle, hoping the medication would soon take effect. I prayed things would go well. The second time the doctor came into the room, Danielle was not asleep, but was too weak from the medication to put up a great fight. I continued to read to her to help keep her calm. Anytime she had to endure difficult, painful procedures, I always prayed and whispered in her ear how much Jesus loved her and continually reminded her to offer her pain for others.

Finally, the medical procedure was done. The blister had been scraped from her face and we had to sit and wait for the results. Patience and waiting was something we had become quite familiar with at the hospital. We spent many hours at the hospital and the clinic waiting for many different reasons. We were able to help the time pass by doing pages in Danielle's workbooks for homeschooling.

After the long wait, we finally received the results clarifying Danielle did in fact have shingles. We had no idea what that hospital stay had in store for us. We were told the shingles would most likely spread. They would cause a great deal of itching, and unlike the chicken pox, they would be on her scalp. They were accompanied by some itching and pain, but I feel she was blessed not to have a really bad case. The shingles combined with heavy chemotherapy made the illness very serious. Her blood counts dropped down to rock bottom. The doctors were not even sure if this was all caused by the shingles or if she was relapsing. Danielle began to have fevers. Blood had to be drawn several times and blood tests were performed to try to identify the cause of the fevers. The doctors were never completely certain of the cause of this secondary infection, but they determined it was probably an infection in her catheter line and not in her blood. She was put on several different antibiotics. Because of the shingles being contagious to the other children at the hospital, Danielle was completely confined in isolation.

She was allowed visitors as long as they had already been exposed to the chicken pox. Unfortunately, not many people came to visit Danielle during this life-threatening time. I don't think they realized how serious this was. At times, I found people's ignorance to be very frustrating, but I continued to remind myself everything was difficult for other people to comprehend. They had their own lives to worry about. If only people could understand, it only takes a phone call or quick text to show some concern. Visits, cards, letters, prayers are other beautiful ways to show love and care.

One thing I have learned from Danielle's illness was how to be more compassionate when others are sick or are in need of some love and prayers. Visiting and reaching out to the sick, elderly and lonely is beautiful Corporal Works of Mercy I have grown to love and appreciate through time. I can now thank God for these types of lonely and suffering experiences we had because they helped me become more considerate and aware of others when they are in need. We must help our neighbors and friends in their sufferings. We all need each other and we all need to feel loved.

Finally, after fourteen days in the hospital, the shingles scabbed over and the fevers ceased. Danielle was then allowed to go home. At home, we had to continue medications for another five days with a home IV. The doctors felt it was important to finish the penicillin she was given. A home nurse came to our home and explained to Philip and me how to prepare and administer the medication. We had to administer the medication around the clock. First, we had to lay out the medicine so it would warm up a little because it was stored in the refrigerator. It seemed to burn if it remained too cold. Then we had to let the pump run for fifteen minutes in one tube, then repeat the process in the other tube.

The night time shots were more irritating because, when finished, it was hard to get back to sleep. Sometimes, Danielle would wake up and she could not go back to sleep either. The penicillin really made Danielle's stomach hurt. It was just another suffering to endure. We were very happy and relieved when this came to an end.

Only about four weeks following this, Danielle was diagnosed once again with an infection in her catheter lines. After speaking with the doctors, it was decided the infection was probably caused by the bath water. Danielle took baths sometimes two or three times a day.

It was something comforting to soothe all her stomach pain caused by the various medications. She had always let her catheter lines hang in the bath water, therefore water must have gotten into the plugged ends. We had been told not to get the patched area wet on her chest. We were never told not to get the tubing wet. I guess we had to learn the hard way.

With this new unnecessary infection, Danielle was angry when she found out she had to stay in the hospital. She had been scheduled to have free pictures donated by Glamour Shots that week. Danielle had really been looking forward to this and it was the third time she would have to cancel. She was screaming, kicking her feet, and banging on the exam table. She repeatedly shouted, "It's not fair, it's not fair!" Danielle had so many disappointments in her life. I felt she had every right to be angry. She needed to let go of her emotions.

This time, Danielle remained in the hospital for about a week. Because of the unknown reason for her fevers, she was again confined to her hospital room. After about a week, we brought her home again with an antibiotic given by a home IV. This was something we became very familiar with. Our house was beginning to take on the appearance of a hospital with all her medications. We have learned God will give grace and will power to get through all challenges in life. Time and time again, we just had to continue to surrender and trust Him.

Summer of Fun

The summer of 1994, Danielle really enjoyed herself. She was glad to be out of school and spend the summer days with her family. She and her sisters always played every day, never complaining of being bored. I thank God over and over again my girls were born so close together. His plan was really a beautiful one.

We spent a lot of our summer days at my parents' house swimming in their pool. Danielle never had a swimming lesson, but she was quite the swimmer. She liked jumping off the diving board and touching the bottom of the nine foot pool and showed to be a natural swimmer. She always swam with her little brother and sisters.

Sometimes, her cousins would also spend a lot of time swimming with us. Danielle grew pretty close to her cousins, Kathryn and Kristen, that summer. They loved playing mermaids together in the pool. Each one of them had an incredible imagination. We also had a lot of big swimming parties on Sundays when the whole family would gather at my parents' house for dinner. The pool was overflowing with grandchildren. I know Danielle really enjoyed living in Oklahoma City and being around a big family. Philip's parents also lived in Oklahoma City, so she got to be with his family also. She really enjoyed having a good time with Philip's brothers. Just like her daddy, they all liked to joke and tease. Danielle was very comfortable with this and teased them also. They were all very special to her.

In the summer, Philip and I both played softball. Danielle enjoyed going to our games, watching us play and also playing with her sisters in the dirt. We bought her a ball glove and began teaching her and Dominique how to play catch. She said the next spring, she wanted to play softball instead of soccer. She was ready to learn something new. Softball has always been my favorite sport and I envisioned Danielle being very good at it also.

During the same summer, we were beginning to sense the end of Danielle's treatment plan. She continued going for her weekly chemotherapy which consisted of leg shots, occasional spinal taps and blood work. However, she still had a difficult time with blood being drawn from her catheter line (a surgically placed infusaport placed under her skin on the top left side of her chest which eliminated the trouble of trying to find a vein in the arm).

It was always a major task to get her to take her shirt off and sit still on my lap while the nurse inserted the needle. Since this particular procedure frightened Danielle so much and caused her so much distress, the doctors decided to remove it. She only had a few months left of chemotherapy treatment, so we felt pretty comfortable with having it removed. She was very happy about this. She made a special request to keep the infusaport as a souvenir of her suffering. She was excited because she saw this as her chemotherapy coming to an end. The catheter reminded her of pain and she wanted it out and gone forever. It also made her self-conscious. Sometimes, people would ask her what she had in her pocket because it bulged out. Then she would have to explain to them what it was and why she had it.

1987 Danielle's Baptism. Philip, Danielle, & Myra

1987 Danielle's Baptism. Godparents, Joe & Dolores with Danielle.

Danielle age 8 months

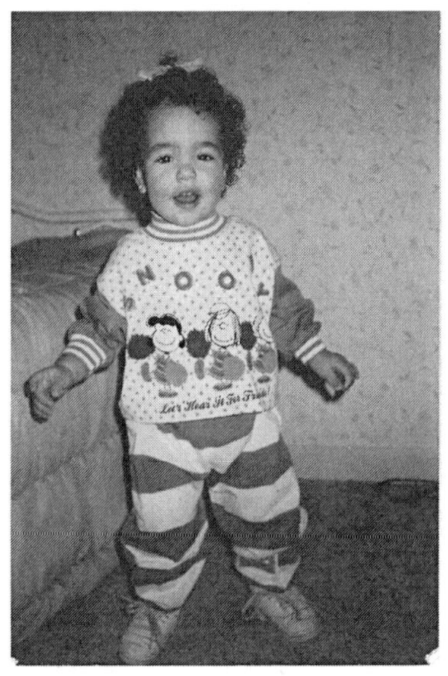

Danielle age 16 months

Danielle age 2 years

1991 Age 4 before diagnosis of leukemia

*1991 Martinez family. L to R Danielle, Myra, Gabrielle, Philip,
& Dominique*

Danielle age 5 years

1993 Danielle, age 6, playing soccer for the Bears

1994 Easter L to R Gabrielle, Danielle, & Dominique

"Jesus on the Cross" by Danielle age 6

1994 Summer fun before relapse. Danielle riding a whale

Danielle & Dominique on their 1st day of school just before her relapse

1994 Age 7 Danielle's Glamour Shots picture following her relapse

Danielle's 7th birthday following her relapse. Danielle is with "La-La, the clown"

Sacrament of Confirmation at Danielle's home

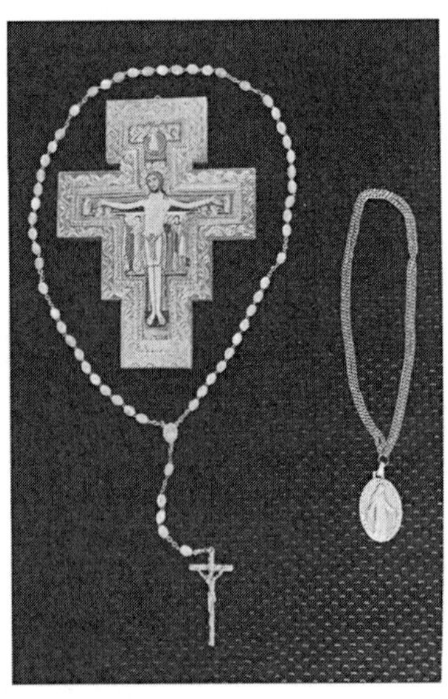

Danielle's Confirmation crucifix and rosary gifts from the Archbishop. Also, the Miraculous Medal necklace that Danielle wore daily throughout the last year of her life.

1994 Make-A-Wish trip to Walt Disneyworld before bone marrow transplant

2018 Martinez family. L to R Michaela, Patrick, Gabrielle, Isabelle, Myra, Malia, Philip, Dominique, Jonathan, & Nathanael

Relapse

In August of 1994, Danielle began first grade at St. James Catholic School. She looked forward to her new school. She was anxious to try out her abilities on the school soccer team and she could not wait to play against her old team and friends from Sacred Heart. She was also happy because she didn't feel alone. That year, her younger sister, Dominique, would start kindergarten at the same school. She enjoyed riding to and from school with Dominique. Their classrooms were right across the hall from each other. This gave them both comfort knowing they were only a short distance away from each other. Each morning, they held hands as Danielle led her sister to her classroom. Dominique and Gabrielle always loved their big sister looking after them. Danielle loved them so much. She often stated, "I am happy I am the one to have leukemia instead of my brother or sisters." She could not bear to see them suffer.

Danielle began making friends right away. I think her shyness attracted people at first, then her silliness took over. She especially enjoyed jumping rope with the second-grade girls. She was very mature for her age and had a September birthday, so she was older in her class. It was not surprising she was making friends with the older girls. Her transition to the new school went smoothly and our lives were about to become normal once again. Or so we thought!

There were only two weeks left of chemotherapy and she would be finished with her two-and-a-half-year treatment plan. She was very excited about this. We all were! We had told her we would have a big mass and party when she was released from care. Her birthday was coming up, so it seemed to be the perfect opportunity to celebrate the release from treatment and her birthday on the same day. The party had started to be planned and Danielle waited with excitement and great anticipation for her big day. She had chosen pink and purple party decorations, since purple was her favorite color. Ironically, the Catholic church issues the color purple to symbolize penance and suffering, while the color pink represents hope.

Once again, our suffering was going to escalate. Danielle came home from school and complained of her leg hurting. I knew she had been jumping rope a lot, so I was not really concerned. As the day went on, she began to limp. I became a little concerned, but I had so much faith that she had been healed, I felt it must be another kind of problem. We had an appointment for her regular chemotherapy treatment the next day, so I decided I would tell the doctor about the pain she was experiencing. At the visit, I told him about her symptoms and he said he would like to wait and see what her blood tests showed before he would become concerned.

This time, after two and a half years of having normal counts, something didn't look right. There were blast cells in her blood indicating there would be trouble! Her doctor told me the combination of the blast cells and leg pain could be indicating her leukemia was returning. Once again, I was alone with Danielle when the doctor gave me the news. Philip was at work since we did not feel Danielle had a serious problem. Remember, we had a lot of faith she had been healed, so the thought of her relapsing didn't really have us overly worried.

The doctor said since tests were already scheduled the following week for release of chemotherapy, it would be better to move them up. If Danielle was relapsing, we needed to know as soon as possible.

I was devastated but remained very calm. I knew a relapse was far worse than the original diagnosis. I know Jesus was carrying me in His arms as I was trying to grasp the difficult situation. If I had not had faith, the drive home alone would have been impossible. I came home and broke the news to Philip. We were both very shocked. How could this be happening? We knew we must not lose our faith or hope. I once heard a priest say it was a sin to lose hope and I've always believed this. We tried to tell ourselves things would be fine. We turned to our faith in God and prayed a lot. It was time to surrender once again.

The night before Danielle's tests, she seemed to have a real nervous energy. She stated, "How can I be relapsing when I feel so good?" Before she went to bed that night, I blessed her with the oil from the crying icon of the Blessed Mother that my mother had given to me. As I prayed over Danielle, she stumbled back. Afterward, she laughed and said it made her feel really dizzy. I have since learned that these tears from the icon were proven to be false. Since Danielle believed they were real with complete faith and love, I don't think it matters if the tears were only pure olive oil or the true tears of Mary, I still feel Danielle's prayers and faith were heard and felt and the blessing I gave was real. We all began praying very fervently.

I think Danielle experienced the same feelings we did. She felt everything would be okay. It was still scary to think she might have relapsed. She had already experienced so much over the past two years and eight months. We waited with confidence and hoped to see what was in store next. If it was a relapse, we knew and trusted Jesus would carry us through, as He always did.

The day came and the tests were performed. After a bone marrow test, spinal tap, bone scan, ultrasound and blood work, the anticipated news was given. Danielle had relapsed with leukemia.

Her bone marrow showed sixty percent leukemia cells. How could this be? Why was this happening? It was so hard to grasp and understand. We had so much faith she had been healed. Again, the Holy Spirit gave us great strength to endure this overwhelming feeling of sadness. We then began trying to accept the reality. I have never felt God caused Danielle's leukemia or her sufferings, but I do feel He allowed them to happen for a greater good.

St. Therese once said, "I believe the devil had received an extra power over me but was not allowed to approach my soul nor my mind except to inspire me with very great fears of certain things for example very simple remedies they tried in vain to make me accept." The Lord was allowing more suffering for some reason, but we did not know why. It was very disappointing, frustrating, exhausting, and frightening because we did not know what Danielle's future held. The only consolation we had was knowing we had withstood other situations with His help, and we knew He would be with us during this one also.

Poor, Danielle; she was just as devastated as we were but did not show much emotion. She seemed to handle the news extraordinarily well. Once she said, "Do you know what my biggest birthday surprise was?"

We said, "No, what, Danielle?"

She replied, "I relapsed. That was the biggest surprise." Danielle knew with the relapse she would have to restart two and one half more years of chemotherapy. However, this time, she would have to have hospital stays of the same durations as the entire treatment plan. She was given only a twenty percent chance of survival. From watching other children at the hospital die from leukemia, she knew by relapsing she might die too. We talked about death with her and she always stated she was not afraid to die. She knew death would take her to Jesus and bring an end to her sufferings. We explained to her there is no more suffering or sadness in Heaven. Probably, the only thing might have bothered her about dying was the thought of leaving her family.

All of our children had a beautiful understanding of death. There is a movie we watched often, titled *The Miracle of Marcelino* in which they learned a lot about death. It was about a little orphan boy, Marcelino, who was raised in a monastery. He was only around the monks and had no mother figure to experience maternal love. As he grew older, he was given many rules to follow. One of the rules was to never go into the attic because there was a man who lived there. Well, curiosity got the best of him and he went into the attic. What he found was a life size crucifix in the corner of the room. Because it was very dark in the attic, Marcelino could not see too well. He thought the man on the cross was the man the monks had told him about. It was actually Jesus, though.

Marcelino befriended Jesus and brought food to Him. Jesus came down from the cross and ate what was given to Him. This went on for days along with conversations. Marcelino discussed his problem of never meeting his mother, while Jesus told him how wonderful His mother was. At the end of the movie, Jesus asked Marcelino if he would like to meet His mother. Marcelino understood what this meant and said yes. Then he laid down and died. After the movie was over, the girls also understood what happened. Jesus allowed the little boy to enter Heaven to be with His heavenly family. For the girls, it was like a preparation for things to come.

Danielle was immediately put on massive doses of steroids. Just as before, they affected her very badly, only worse this time. The stomach cramps she endured were excruciatingly painful. The kids at school politely asked her why her cheeks were so chubby. She explained to them it was caused by the medication. As expected, since the chemotherapy was so very powerful, she lost all of her thick, brown curly hair. It took less than a week to lose every strand. Danielle was a little girl who loved long, beautiful hair. Once she said, "I wish I had long hair all the way down to my ankles."

I said, "Then you would trip on it."

She answered, "No, I wouldn't. I would hold it." Unfortunately, she was unable to see this long, beautiful hair she had dreamed of. We all watched as Danielle's hair traumatically fell out by the handful. It started as a bald spot and each time I brushed it, more and more came out. We would find her hair everywhere. She began to look as though she had experienced a nuclear war. As I brushed her hair, I had to put a trash can next to me so I Could throw away the piles. I would sit behind her, crying silently so she could not hear me as I threw her hair in the trash. It was also very hard on Philip and on her sisters. It really seemed to bother her youngest sister, Gabrielle, who was almost five years old. Gabrielle kept staring at Danielle. It took her some time to get used to it. She was comforted to know it would grow back. Looking at Danielle without her hair was a constant reminder of her leukemia. Remember, before when she was first diagnosed, I had prayed she would keep her hair as a sign she would be healed.

For the first time, I began to wonder if physical healing was part of God's plan. Sometimes I would reflect back and remember my consecration to God, entrusting Danielle to His Divine plan for her life. I knew I must surrender everything to His will.

Grace was given to Danielle and she handled the loss with a supernatural strength. What was especially amazing to me was she never complained or cried once about losing her hair, and I know it must have been a painful loss. Once she stated, "Oh, well, it's just hair. It will grow back." Rather than feeling sorry for herself, she seemed to be the one comforting us instead. When she went out in public, she always wore a hat and scarf. We bought her many different hats and scarves to help her feel more comfortable. Around the house, she did not like wearing her hat or scarf. She found them to be uncomfortable. Once, when her uncle Joe came to visit her at the hospital, she did not feel like wearing a hat, but she did anyway so it wouldn't be uncomfortable for him. She thought it would hurt him to see her without hair.

Her first grade at St. James School was very kind to her about her new appearance. They thought it was cool she had hats to match the different colors of her school uniform. They never made fun of her or tried to pull off her hat like I feared. Instead of becoming unpopular or someone to be scared of, she seemed to be more popular than ever. Often, when she came to school, she was greeted with big hugs from a lot of the students. Many people enjoyed the love Danielle generated. She was always so very kind to everyone, even to those whom no one seemed to like. When I taught her Jesus wanted us to love everyone, she not only listened to the teaching; she practiced it well. Sharing love with others came naturally for her.

Many times, Danielle missed school because she was in too much pain and nauseated from the side effects of the steroids. Sitting all day at a hard school desk was unbearable. Sometimes, she spent the day in bed moaning in pain. We all suffered with Danielle as we listened to her in agonizing pain. There was nothing we could do for her but pray. She spent a lot of time lying in bed listening to soft music, mostly religious songs. The music seemed to help her be at peace and better endure her great suffering. Even a ride in the car was difficult. She had to lay down in the car everywhere we went. At church, she just laid in the pew. I remember giving her baths to try to soothe her, but she would sit with her head lying on the side of the bathtub. It was difficult for all of us.

Because she was missing so much school, I started to inquire and research about the Seton home schooling program. This Catholic home school was accredited. She was currently in first grade at St. James School, but I always felt she was capable of doing a grade higher. Therefore, I ordered the Seton school program for the second grade. It was challenging and we had to send our work to be graded on a quarterly basis.

Danielle did very well and home schooling was not nearly as difficult as I had expected it to be. Because she was home schooling, she was able to do a lot of her school work at home, in the hospital and while we waited in the hematology clinic. She excelled in all subjects, but history and English were her favorites. She was able to complete one semester of second grade with Seton Homeschool. She made all As. We were all very proud of her. Her home school work and books helped keep her busy and her mind occupied during all those times of waiting at the hospital clinic.

I am so thankful I was able to teach Danielle. Philip also helped with her math and science work. This gave us both an opportunity to spend more time with her. I am very grateful for the closeness that was created by home schooling. It took me a couple of years and prayers of discernment before I felt the calling to homeschool our other children. Surprisingly, Dominique and Gabrielle asked me to homeschool them. Homeschool was a very positive experience and an incredible blessing for our whole family. By homeschooling, I was able to increase the faith and knowledge of my children and strengthen their morals. By being home together, they grew closer to each other. Eventually, I would go on to homeschool for over 15 years until God called me to other things.

Though Danielle liked her homeschool books, she still longed to go back to her friends and teachers at St. James. At the time, we did not know about all the wonderful home school groups available. She wanted things to be as they were before her relapse. At times, I wish I would have always homeschooled her, but I feel by keeping her in St. James School she was able to touch many more lives in our Catholic community. She was outspoken about her faith. She was a true evangelist. One first grade mother said Danielle used to carry on very deep conversations with the other children on the school playground. Usually, she did not feel well enough to jump around and play, so she stayed sitting down at recess time.

She would sit and talk with her friends. Once, she told them she would not live as long as they would. She said she would go to Heaven before them, but not to worry because she would always be with them, watching over them. I found this to be incredible, but not too surprising that Danielle would say this. I had spoken to her about death on several occasions. At this time, we had not yet told her she might die, but she knew the relapse increased her chance of death. All she had to do was look around her at Children's Hospital to see death was real.

Even though Danielle believed she had a good chance of dying, she always remained happy. Nothing disturbed her peace. It was her faith that kept her strong. I feel only a soul with great faith and love for God would handle life and death in the way she did. God filled her with His grace. Heaven was explained to Danielle on many occasions, especially after her cancer relapse.

I always explained to Danielle that Heaven was a beautiful place God had planned for those who loved Him. It is so beautiful, if we saw it, we would not be able to describe it in words. I explained we suffered here on earth, but in Heaven there was no more pain and suffering. She knew there would be no more sickness in Heaven. I also assured her Heaven was a happy, joyful place and there was no sadness there (except watching the souls on earth who lived in evil and sin). Danielle understood that in Heaven she would be surrounded by Jesus, Mary, all the angels and the great Communion of Saints. She stated many times she was not afraid of dying. We had explained to her Heaven was better than anything she had ever experienced on earth. It was more joyful than we could imagine. She loved God so very much. I believe she looked forward to the day when our whole family would be joined together in God's heavenly kingdom.

I never told Danielle that Heaven was a giant toy land or a place she could do whatever she wanted. The image she had set in her mind was very holy and not of this earth. Heaven did not need to be materialistic in order for her to desire it. I have found too many parents explain Heaven to their children like a fairy tale, and I see it as totally unnecessary. Children love the truth. I explained to Danielle that in Heaven, she would no longer have a need for things of this earth, such as toys or even people of this earth. She believed and understood that in Heaven our family would be together, but it would not be the same earthly way we shared life here on earth.

Besides Heaven, Danielle also understood Purgatory and Hell very well. She knew the souls in Purgatory needed and longed for her prayers and sufferings. I taught her all souls in Purgatory would eventually reach Heaven and would be saved. She understood Purgatory was a time of purification-a place in which souls needed to stay in order to cleanse themselves to become holier before entering the Divine Presence of God. She never questioned this concept.

I also taught Danielle the poor souls in Purgatory could not help themselves, but we could help them and they could help us with prayers. At prayer time, at the end of the day, sometimes, it was Danielle who reminded me to pray for the souls in Purgatory. I truly believe she had a great love for the poor souls. Once, I heard more souls are saved on Christmas Day than any other day of the year. This might help explain why Danielle had to suffer the most severely on the last Christmas of her life. I told Danielle on several occasions one day, when she reached Heaven, she would be able to see and meet all the souls she helped through her prayers and suffering. I explained to her they would be eternally grateful to her. This always brought a smile to her face, even when she was experiencing intense pain.

Even though Danielle was a child, I did not shy away from teaching her about the evil of Satan and Hell. I explained to Danielle the souls in Hell are there because they chose to be. They chose to hate God and they had no desire to be with Him. Danielle knew about the fall of Lucifer and the other bad angels. She knew and believed Hell was something real, but also something we should not fear, if we are full of the love of God. Once, I told Danielle the Devil hated being called Lucifer since God gave him this name meaning 'Angel of Light'. After I told her this, she enjoyed calling him Lucifer. She deliberately wanted to show him her rejection of him. She showed no signs of fear for him or his fellow demons. I believe that spiritual awareness of Heaven and Hell gave her a stronger understanding of the power in her daily sufferings and sacrifices offered to help the souls who needed God's special grace.

Besides afterlife, Danielle was also told about Marian Apparitions. We have a movie on the Apparition of Our Lady of Fatima she enjoyed watching very much. In the movie, the visionaries are allowed by our Blessed Mother to see a glimpse of Hell. Danielle believed this and other apparitions. On several occasions, she stated how she would love for Mary or Jesus to appear to her while she was awake rather than just a dream. She said she would not be afraid. She truly longed to be with them and enjoy their beautiful, holy presence.

Danielle's Seventh Birthday

Not long after the relapse of leukemia, we went forward with Danielle's birthday celebration. This special party was originally planned to be a grand celebration for her seventh birthday along with a special mass of Thanksgiving for the termination of all her chemotherapy treatments and declaring Danielle was healed from her leukemia.

The celebration day had finally arrived! On 17 September 1994, we celebrated Danielle and the gift of her life. This time, our prayer intentions were a bit different. She had looked forward to this special day for so long. At the time of the party, the steroids had already begun to take their cruel effect. We hoped and prayed she could tolerate the party since she was suffering so much with stomach pain from the high volume of steroids and chemotherapy drugs.

Many friends and relatives came to the birthday celebration. We began with a mass celebrated by Fr George Pupius at St. Andrew's Church. Danielle felt so bad she spent most of the beautiful mass lying down in the front pew of the church. She wore a festive, black dress with brightly colored polka dots. Since by this time, she had lost all of her hair, she wore a headscarf and little polka dot hat which matched her dress.

After the mass, friends and family joined us for a big party on the church lawn and pavilions. There were lots of games, prizes, face painting, a moonwalk, and even a clown. It was the same sweet pink haired 'La La' clown who had visited Danielle at the hospital when she was first diagnosed with leukemia. This time, however, 'La La' was able to connect with Danielle and bring a smile to her face.

Sadly, Danielle felt too terrible to play the planned games. She spent almost the whole afternoon sitting on a lawn chair unwrapping all her wonderful presents. I made her a birthday cake and decorated it in her favorite color, purple. The temptation of fun became too great for her, though. She wanted to participate in all the fun, so she got into the moonwalk. She ended up crying because it made her feel sick. I had to carry her back to her lawn chair. I felt so disappointed for her. Even though she could not participate much at the party, she still managed to be very happy and enjoy herself. Seeing all her friends and family who loved her and supported her meant more to her than anything.

Danielle was truly blessed to have so many people love her and pray for her. It was always heartwarming and amazing to see the amount of people who continued to pray for Danielle throughout her illness. I really feel through the Sacraments and through the prayers of others, Danielle was given a supernatural grace and strength to endure all her sufferings peacefully. I am sincerely grateful for all those who prayed so much and cared so greatly!

Camp Watonga

In the same fall of 1994, we were invited to camp by the Oklahoma Children's Cancer Association to spend a day of fun in Watonga, Oklahoma with our family. The Watonga camp was hosted by the Watonga firefighters. The weekend of camp, Philip had to be at a chiropractic seminar, so sadly, he couldn't attend. I did not want Danielle to miss this opportunity, so I asked my mom and dad to go with me and the kids. I am very thankful for that great experience. We all had a good time, especially Danielle. Unfortunately, Danielle's stomach was hurting and she felt very bad, but she still managed to have fun. My parents and I were overwhelmed by the care and generosity of the Watonga community. It was obvious these people truly cared for the children as shown with their generous outpouring of love.

While at the camp, Danielle did not feel well enough to go horseback riding or participate in some of the other fun activities, but she was able to lie back and enjoy the fishing. She had always wanted to fish and this was her big chance. While the children waited with their fishing lines in the water, the volunteers were out on the lake in their boats. They were busy secretly placing prize winning catfish on the end of the children's lines. When Danielle rolled her line in with a big catfish, she was super excited! A beautiful smile grew on her face, I had not seen for a long time. Her sisters and little brother were having a blast also.

This turned out to be a very pleasant experience for all of us. Again, the heartfelt love shared was overwhelming. It was also on that special day that Danielle was able to take her mind off her horrible suffering and enjoy herself a little bit. I will always be thankful to the Oklahoma Children's Cancer Association and the free fun times volunteers gave to Danielle and all the other children who were suffering from cancer. One of the many things I had learned from Danielle's illness was how to love and care more for others. I learned this through the example of so many caring hearts.

Sharing in the Eucharist Regularly

After Danielle's relapse, I took her to see Fr John McMenamin at St. James Church. I asked for permission for Danielle to receive Communion regularly since her relapse put her into a life-threatening situation and she understood her faith so well. I taught her a lot about the Sacraments of Confession and the Eucharist. She had a beautiful and full understanding of Jesus' presence in the Blessed Sacrament. Fr John questioned Danielle very thoroughly. Afterward, he determined she did believe and understood Jesus was in the Eucharist. She had always had a good understanding about how the bread does not become Jesus until after the prayers of consecration. Fr John gave permission, therefore, on the following Sunday, she could begin receiving the Sacrament of Holy Communion regularly. As we were leaving, he also picked and gave her some roses growing on a rose bush outside the rectory.

At first, Danielle did not realize Fr John was giving her special permission to receive the Eucharist. When we got into the car, I explained to her she could now receive Jesus in Holy Communion on a regular basis. She was thrilled! She smiled a great big smile and tears filled her eyes. This time, they were tears of pure joy, tears I would love to have bottled up and saved forever. Then, looking down at the roses, she said, "This rose reminds me of Jesus and how He suffered. The thorns remind me of the crown He wore on His head."

I was in awe of her beautiful thoughts and meditation. She always had such a wonderful understanding of Jesus' sorrowful passion. Even happy, joyful times reminded her of His sufferings. Rather than thinking of her own sufferings, she would sometimes think of His first. I always reminded her many saints wanted to share in the suffering of Jesus. They would have loved being in her place. She understood with such spiritual wisdom that could have only come from a special gift from the Holy Spirit.

After Danielle returned home from our meeting with Fr John, she immediately got a vase and filled it with water for her beautiful roses. One of the roses was only a bud, still wrapped in its green shell. Each day, she waited anxiously for the little rose to bloom. Finally, growing impatient, she began to help the rose along by peeling away the green. Within a couple of days, I was amazed watching this little rose as it came into full bloom! I had never seen roses survive as long as those roses did.

The following Sunday could not arrive soon enough. Since this was not actually Danielle's first Holy Communion, no party was planned. No one in the church even knew of this special day for her. She didn't even have the honor of going up first to receive Jesus. No announcement was made, no fancy white dress was worn, no party was given and no relatives were present. This was exactly as my first Holy Communion was made.

Unlike Danielle, though, I remember complaining for years of what I thought was my simple first Holy Communion day. Instead of a day that was totally given to Jesus, I was expecting something for myself. I wanted to be the center of attention. Danielle was not like me at all. She never once complained of receiving Jesus quietly, in complete humility. Instead, she gave her special day with total love and adoration to Jesus. She was so happy! She did not need the attention of others. She only desired Jesus. Her sister, Dominique, told me many times Danielle would tell her how she wished she could receive the Eucharist every day.

Once Danielle was able to receive Holy Communion regularly, she really developed a great desire to attend mass as often as possible. Besides regular Sunday mass, sometimes, she would ask to go with Philip or me during the weekdays. Even though she was not a morning person, she would give up sleeping late on Saturday mornings so she could attend mass with Philip. She loved receiving Jesus in the Eucharist. Sadly, Danielle was never able to receive the Sacrament of Reconciliation.

Fr John felt because she was so young it would be best to wait. He said there was no hurry. Danielle often commented she wanted to make her first Confession, so we asked on several different occasions. It seemed obstacles kept getting in the way and it was put off for one reason or another. She continued to read her book on the Sacrament of Confession, though, because she felt certain she would get to confess her sins through the Sacrament someday. Confession was something she was ready for and really desired, but never was able to do physically; however, I know she already did so in her heart with her desire.

Finding a Donor

During this time of Danielle's relapse, we were told she would only have two options of treatment. We could just continue with her regular treatment, but she would only have a twenty percent chance for survival. We were told a bone marrow transplant could increase her chance of survival to fifty percent. We were already experienced with the hospital stays, so we needed to research more about the bone marrow transplant to make a good, informed decision. We made an appointment to meet with the bone marrow doctor at Children's Hospital in Oklahoma City. He sat us down at a conference table and explained to us very graphically the many side effects and risks of the bone marrow transplant. All sounded very frightening and horrific, but we were given some hope in the thought of Danielle having a better chance of surviving.

On the way back home, Philip and I both felt sick to our stomachs and just wanted to cry at the thought of all the gruesome things Danielle would have to suffer with if we elected to have a bone marrow transplant. We had a lot of doubts about whether this was what we really wanted. How could we choose and elect to have our little girl suffer so much? We prayed a lot about it and decided if God wanted

Danielle to have a bone marrow transplant, then he would find her an exact donor match. We put the problem and decision in His hands and trusted His will.

We would do our part also. We put out a message to all our relatives that a match needed to be found. Not only did relatives volunteer, but so did many of our friends and acquaintances. The love and caring by so many people was beautiful and overwhelming. All of our children endured the blood test to determine if any of them could match Danielle's bone marrow. Unfortunately, none of them matched, but they were all very brave and not one of them even cried. I believe this was because of their great desire to help Danielle. They would have endured anything if they thought it would save their big sister's life.

We continued to pray for an exact donor match to be found. Danielle's bone marrow type was entered into a computer and a search began through the national bone marrow donor registry. Philip and I decided if an exact match was not found, then we would not allow Danielle to have a transplant. There would be too many risks involved and her chances of cure would be even less. We just had to wait to see what God had in store for us, again trusting in His plan.

Another Means of Suffering

While waiting for a donor match to be found, we decided to have another type of catheter line placed in Danielle's chest called an outer Hickman catheter. This would require a surgery to place a small tube into one of the veins in the chest region. On the outside of her body, an open wound would allow this tube to exit. It was needed for Danielle to prevent skin punctures she would have with blood tests and the administration of chemotherapy. Also, if we decided to have the bone marrow transplant, the catheter would be mandatory. Therefore, we decided to have the Hickman catheter placed. We thought it would be a relief from some of her suffering, but instead, it turned out to be another way for her to suffer.

Since the catheter left an open wound in her chest, we had to change the outer covering with new, clean, sterile bandages twice a week. If we did not do this procedure regularly, she would be at high risk for infection and the catheter would have to be removed. We knew at first the patch changes would be time-consuming, but we had no idea of the pain and suffering it would bring.

First, there was the smell of alcohol. Danielle developed a hatred for the odor because it reminded her of the hospital and of all the pain she had endured during her stays. Then, the area around the catheter had become very tender from all the sticky tape and it burned when alcohol and other medications were applied. Removing the large, sticky patch was a big struggle in itself. She did not want help removing it. She always wanted to do it herself. She almost always cried as she worked at peeling it off her delicate skin. Sometimes, this alone could take ten minutes or more. It was a physical pain for her, but it was an emotional pain for us.

Philip and I were always with her during her patch changes, except when she was in the hospital. Philip did all the dressing changes as I sat and watched, trying to be a support and give comfort. One time, we all had such a struggle, by the time we had finished, all three of us were crying. Philip and I hated to see Danielle suffer so much through this. While some children have no problem changing these dressings on their catheters, it was a great suffering and miserable experience for Danielle. She absolutely hated it and dreaded it every time.

Danielle could not be submerged in water or get her catheter area wet. That meant absolutely no swimming and limited her bath time, which was where she liked to play. She could no longer lay down in the bathtub, which she loved to do, or take baths with her sisters for fear they would splash.

One time, when her little brother, Nathanael, was playing with her while she was taking a bath, he reached into the water and playfully splashed her. She was so upset, not with him, but at the fact she got her patch wet and it would have to be changed. I felt so sorry for her as she sat there in the tub crying. She did not want to get out because she knew, when she did, her dressings would have to be changed immediately.

Needless to say, Danielle suffered a lot from changing the dressings on her Hickman catheter. The positive thing about the catheter was medications and blood work could be done straight through the catheter without jabbing her skin with another needle. It was very hard on us, but it was much easier for the nurses.

Even though we had the catheter put in, there were still a few occasions she had to have blood drawn from her veins. This was sheer torture for her. On one such occasion, four different nurses had to take turns attempting to find her vein. I held her in my lap while she held out her arm and cried the entire time. It was so hard putting her through this, but we had no choice. The only consolation she had was knowing by offering her pain she could help others who were in Purgatory. I was very proud of her when she was able to bravely hold out her arm and not move during frightening procedures. I did not mind if she screamed and cried, but holding still was very important.

When she was scared, it always gave her more comfort and security to sit on my lap during painful procedures. I always prayed for her and for guidance and wisdom for the nurses and doctors during difficult tests. Sometimes, I felt God allowed extra pain and difficulties because Danielle was a victim soul. Her soul was willing to suffer for the benefit of others. If someone would have asked Danielle if she wanted to suffer, I'm sure she probably would have said, "No, I would rather feel good and be healthy like other normal kids." But I feel if a person had the ability to ask her soul if it was willing to suffer for others, it would have responded with a definite 'yes', because her soul had such a great love for God and for the suffering souls of others.

One night, Danielle and Philip stayed up until about 12:30 a.m. watching an old, black and white movie about St. Bernadette called, *The Song of Bernadette*. At one point in the movie, one of the superior nuns admonished Bernadette, because she was limping during prayer time. When taken to her room to discuss it further, the nun was obviously jealous because Bernadette was chosen to see the Virgin Mary and not her. She said she had experienced much more suffering and should be more deserving of the apparition. Bernadette apologized, then said maybe she does have some suffering to offer. She lifted the skirt of her habit and showed a large tumor was growing on her leg. She had never complained or told anyone, she just offered it to God.

When this occurred, Philip asked Danielle what she thought. She said it would be very hard. She said this half-laughing with a funny tone in her voice. It was like she wanted to, but was not sure if she could. Philip told her, like St. Bernadette, she offered her pain very well. A special word of wisdom from Our Lady of Lourdes to St. Bernadette was, "I cannot promise to make you happy in this world, but only in the next." This movie was such a beautiful example and message for Danielle in helping her with her own suffering.

A Perfect Match

After Danielle's birthday, we continued to wait for a bone marrow donor to be found. We had prayed a great deal that God would choose to heal her with a bone marrow transplant and He would find an exact match for her. We also prayed, if she could not be healed through a transplant, a match would not be found. Then, one day, we were called by the bone marrow transplant coordinator. She told us a match had in fact been found. At first, the donor showed to be one antigen away from matching Danielle's marrow. After further testing, he showed all six of these antigens matched Danielle's exactly. They re-tested to make sure this was accurate. Every test showed a perfect match. Since all antigens matched, we felt sure this must have been the answer to our prayers.

We were not allowed to know anything about Danielle's bone marrow donor except for his age and sex. He was also not allowed to know anything about Danielle except she was a seven-year-old girl who had relapsed with leukemia. He was told the transplant could help save her life. He was truly a very generous soul who I am thankful for and have a lot of admiration for his willingness to suffer for Danielle's life. We all began praying for him when we decided to go forward with the procedure. Danielle was also very thankful for her kind and caring donor. I am sure she still prays for him.

Danielle went through many tests in preparation for the transplant. The doctors needed these to confirm her body was physically fit and able to endure the battle of a bone marrow transplant. Other than leukemia, Danielle had always been very healthy and physically fit. In fact, she had not even seen a doctor or taken a prescription drug for a whole year or more before her diagnosis of leukemia. While under treatment, she was rarely sick with anything except illnesses caused by chemotherapy.

Come Holy Spirit

Besides the Sacraments of Holy Communion and the Anointing of the Sick, I kept feeling there was more Danielle needed in order to help her on her jagged road of suffering. We knew, with a bone marrow transplant, she had a fifteen percent chance of dying following the procedure. We also knew the transplant would cause awful suffering, worse than anything she had ever experienced. We depended on God's grace to carry us.

My Catholic friend, Michelle, asked me if I had ever given thought to having Danielle Confirmed. She told me, as far as she knew, a person could receive the Sacrament of Confirmation if their life was in danger regardless of their age. She encouraged me to find out more, which I felt was an inspiration from the Holy Spirit. That night, I laid awake, thinking about calling our parish priest to see about the Confirmation for Danielle. As I was contemplating this, Danielle began crying out loudly in her room calling, "Mommy, Mommy!" I immediately went into her bedroom to check on her. She told me, "Something is bothering me! I don't know what it is, but it won't go away!"

I asked her if she was having a bad dream and she said, "No, I don't know what it is." I told her to wait a minute and

I would get the holy water to bless her and her bedroom. After blessing her and the bedroom, she calmly asked me if I would stay in her room until she fell asleep. She slept peacefully for the rest of the night. I began to feel certain Confirmation was what Danielle really needed. It seemed strange, and more than coincidental, I was thinking thoughts of arranging her to be Confirmed and Danielle was being disturbed by an evil presence at the same moment. I knew in my heart Satan really hated this idea of Danielle obtaining the beautiful Sacrament that would give her so much grace to help endure her sufferings and death. After that incident, I was more determined to help get Danielle Confirmed in her Catholic faith as soon as possible. If the devil wanted to fight, I was ready for the challenge!

The next day, I called our parish priest, Fr James Kastner, at St. James Catholic Church. He told me there should be no problem in Confirming Danielle. In fact, he took it a step further and said he would like Archbishop Eusebius Beltran to give Danielle the Sacrament of Confirmation! He felt this would be more meaningful and very special for Danielle. When he called Archbishop Beltran and explained Danielle's situation, the Archbishop said he would love to administer the Sacrament. It was arranged for Archbishop Beltran to come to our house to administer the Sacrament of Confirmation to her. We were all very excited and awaited the day with great anticipation!

Finally, on 1 December 1994, Archbishop Beltran, Fr Kastner, and Fr McMenamin came to our home for Danielle's Confirmation. Danielle chose her godfather, Uncle Joe Martinez, to be her Confirmation sponsor. After much thought and prayer, she decided on St. Therese of

Lisieux, the Little Flower, as her Confirmation patron saint. Since Danielle had asked Saint Therese many times to pray for her, she felt closest to her. She also seemed to know the most about St. Therese and her life and very much admired her. St. Therese once stated at her own Confirmation she received the strength to suffer, for soon afterward, the martyrdom of her soul was about to commence. I believe this was also true for Danielle.

Danielle was wearing a navy blue, print skirt with a matching beige shirt. She wore a navy blue silk scarf on her head with her navy blue hat. She was also wearing angel earrings and a necklace with a crucifix. Hanging around her neck was a large, blessed Miraculous Medal which had been given to her by a man named Rod from our church, after her relapse. The medal was special to her and she always wore it. She knew the story of St. Catherine Laboure of the Miraculous Medal, which I believe helped contribute to her love and devotion for the medal. Now Philip wears this special medal every day.

That evening, the atmosphere seemed to radiate with God's love. The presence of the Holy Spirit was very strong that night and it was He who was piercing the very depths of Danielle's soul. According to the Catechism of the Catholic Church, "It is evident from its celebration the effect of the Sacrament of Confirmation is the full outpouring of the Holy Spirit as once granted to the apostles on the day of Pentecost. From this fact, Confirmation brings an increase and deepening of Baptismal grace." It could easily be seen by looking at Danielle's face that she had a new fire burning within.

After her Confirmation, Archbishop Beltran presented Danielle with two beautiful gifts. First, he gave her a San Damiano crucifix from Bethlehem that still hangs in the entry way of our home.

He asked Danielle if she had ever heard of Bethlehem. She nodded her head yes, and received the wooden crucifix with a big, soft smile. She held it in her hands and gazed at it with great love in her eyes.

Then, Archbishop Beltran reached into his pocket and pulled out a beautiful, white rosary with a gold crucifix and gold chain. While showing Danielle the beautiful rosary, he asked her if she had ever heard of John Paul II. Again, she nodded her head with a great big smile. He gave her the rosary and told her it had been given to him by Pope John Paul II and it had the Pope's blessing. I could tell Danielle was extremely happy and this rosary really meant a great deal to her.

Next, my mother gave Danielle a statue of her patron, St. Therese of Lisieux. Danielle seemed to be very happy with the statue as well. She was very excited about her special gifts, but even more so about her new name. I could see and feel Danielle's happiness when Archbishop Beltran Confirmed her, calling her by the name Danielle Therese. Following the Confirmation, Danielle always signed her name as Danielle Therese.

After everyone had left, Danielle went immediately into her room, climbed up into her bunk bed, and took a large picture of the 101 Dalmations off her wall. This picture hung directly over the head of Danielle's bed. She replaced the picture with her new, beautiful San Damiano crucifix. She had such a love and understanding of Jesus on the cross.

It did not surprise us when Danielle showed this act of love and faith. Her sweet example of faith and love for God always appeared to us as extraordinary.

Danielle's new gifts were additions to an already spiritually decorated bedroom. On the wall next to Danielle's bed was the picture of the Infant Jesus of Prague and an icon of the Blessed Mother Mary holding the Infant Jesus. Danielle's godfather, Uncle Joe, had given her a collection of beautifully painted plates of various pictures and titles of the Blessed Mother that took up two shelves in the room. The girls' room still looked like a girls room with all the toys, but at the same time took on the appearance of a small shrine with all their religious and blessed items. I feel this gave them all peace and comfort as they suffered.

Danielle's cancer was very difficult for her little sisters. They had been ripped apart from her by the cancer, constantly being separated by the hospital stays and having to witness Danielle's crying and suffering. They were strongly bonded and suffered much together. All the siblings continue to carry the cross of losing a big sister, even the ones who never got to meet her and know her personally.

After the Confirmation, Philip and I took the kids out to eat pizza to celebrate. When we arrived at the restaurant, it was obvious Danielle was glowing. How could she not be? She was so full of the Holy Spirit and still smelled of Chrism Oil. This was definitely one of the happiest events of her life!

Danielle was not suffering during this time because she had been taken off of chemotherapy for the past four weeks to prepare her body for the bone marrow transplant. The stomach pains, burning throat, as well as other sufferings, were temporarily removed. I am so thankful she did not have to suffer physically during this joyful time in her life. I am sure this is the way God had planned for it to be, so the timing was perfectly God's time.

Later, at the restaurant, Danielle and I were at the table alone while Philip and the others were ordering the pizza. Danielle had brought her new rosary with her. It made her so happy! As we sat at the table, Danielle gazed upon it and said, "This rosary is so beautiful. It reminds me of the Pope. It is white and gold, just like him." She then looked at me smiling and said, "I love you." I will cherish this moment for the rest of my life because Danielle did not initiate the phrase, 'I love you', very often, so it was very meaningful. When she said this, I could see and feel she was thanking me for the wonderful evening filled with God's love. She knew and understood well her Confirmation was very powerful and would be one of the most important days of her life. She would not have traded that beautiful blessed day for anything. I reminded her she was now full of the Holy Spirit, just as the apostles at Pentecost. Danielle loved this idea and what a disciple she became!

She let us know that her new beautiful rosary increased her desire to pray the rosary even more. She felt it was a great encouragement in her prayer life. I would like to appreciate the rosary as much as she did, but she had such a love so innocent and humble. Her soul was so pure and her heart burned with God's radiating love. I feel her great love for God showered graces upon our whole family. We all benefited from her prayers and redemptive suffering.

Trip to Disney World

After Danielle relapsed, the children's oncology unit encouraged us to contact the Make-a-Wish Foundation to request getting Danielle a wish. A woman from the foundation came to our home to talk with Danielle. Since, Danielle was very shy, she only answered questions by smiling or nodding her head. Before this visit, we had already talked to Danielle about some different places she could go. As a family, we all decided Disney World in Orlando, Florida, would be a fun family trip. Danielle was very excited at the thought of it! Since our immediate finances were already strained, it was a place we never dreamed we could go and take our family.

The Make-a-Wish Foundation began making arrangements for the trip right away. We planned the trip for the first week of December. We knew, at this time, Danielle would be off chemotherapy to prepare her body for the bone marrow transplant. This would mean Danielle would be feeling better and close to normal. We began planning and getting excited about our family dream trip. It seemed too good to be true!

However, due to conflicts with the procedures for the transplant, we found out Danielle's bone marrow procedure would be scheduled for 16 December. She was required to check into the hospital on 7 December, so she could begin radiation treatments on 8 December, the Feast of the Immaculate Conception. In order for us to be back in time, we would have to cut our trip one day short. We planned to leave for Disney World on 3 December, and return on 7 December. That same day, she would be admitted into Children's Hospital in Oklahoma City.

Since the transplant date was set for Dominique's sixth birthday, 16 December 1994, we had to begin to figure out a way for Danielle to still enjoy Christmas and her sister's birthday. It was not our normal tradition, but as soon as Thanksgiving was over, we put up our Christmas tree in our home. We then made arrangements to celebrate Dominique's birthday early. Dominique did not mind this at all, though it was hard for her on her birthday to fully understand why we were not celebrating with another party.

The following week, we celebrated our Christmas together before leaving on our trip to Disney World. We wrote Santa Clause a letter and told him our difficult situation. This was how he knew to make an early stop at our house. I am so glad we were able to do this. It meant so much to share some of Christmas joy together as a family. We knew Danielle's siblings would not be allowed to go into her room at the hospital. We wanted them to be with her when she opened her Christmas presents. We also knew Danielle would probably be feeling bad at Christmas and would possibly be too weak to even open a present. But for now, we wanted to forget about our sufferings and have fun on Danielle's wish trip.

The day for us to leave could not come soon enough. The girls had flown on a plane when they were babies, so for them, this would be like flying for the first time. We had to get up very early to make our flight. First, we stopped in Dallas, then on to Orlando. Needless to say, the kids were super excited! They did very well on the flight, which was a blessing.

We arrived in Orlando in the afternoon. A couple from the Make-a-Wish Foundation met us at the gate and escorted us to get our luggage and rental car. They showed us how to get to where we were going to stay, which was an amazing amusement park in itself. It was incredibly nice!

The place was called 'Give Kids the World'. This was a magnificent little village, especially made for children with life-threatening problems. Each family stayed in a cottage, which was very similar to a nice, two-bedroom house. In the village area, there was a spectacular castle made just for the children to play in. All the toys and special effects in this castle were unbelievable! Danielle liked the wishing well that talked. Every time someone dropped a coin in the well, it made a different sound. It was so nice to see her so happy. There was also a computer where she and her sister spent a long time playing. Everything about the castle was fascinating. We were told it cost over two million dollars to build and it had all been funded by donations.

Outside the castle was a beautiful, hand-carved carousel from Holland. It was a free ride the kids could ride throughout the day. Danielle really thought this was wonderful. The carousel even had special handicap spaces for children who had to be in a wheelchair.

Each morning, we ate a nice buffet breakfast at the village Gingerbread House. It was as wonderful on the inside as on the outside. Outside, it looked just like a gingerbread house. Inside, it had little, red tables and chairs. The tables had glass tops with red and white peppermints inlayed in the glass. If you looked up, all around, you would see dolls from all over the world.

Since Danielle loved porcelain dolls, she was fascinated looking at them. All the people who worked there were volunteers. They were all very courteous and gave us anything we needed. The whole place seemed surrounded by love. Danielle wore a button every day we were there to let everyone know she was special. That button was her ticket to free rides and royal treatment. It meant so much to us to see her feel so good and have such a good time. After all the sufferings she went through, I am so thankful she finally got to experience some happier moments.

Each day, a different Walt Disney character visited the village. Danielle again was very shy and would not talk with them, but she did enjoy having her picture made with the different characters. Her favorites were Mickey and Minnie Mouse. When we started to go to the parks, our first visit was to the Magic Kingdom at Walt Disney World.

We all had a great time there and considered this place our favorite of the whole trip. We were told if Danielle would ride in a wheelchair she would not have to wait in lines for the rides and we would all be assured a good seat. Unfortunately, Danielle did not think this was such a great idea. It was too humiliating for her. We could not convince her sisters to ride either. Of course, if Danielle did not approve, then they did not approve either. They always looked up to Danielle and respected her decisions. We also visited the Epcot Center, Universal Studios, MGM Studios and SeaWorld. After a lot of walking, Danielle realized the wheelchair just might be the better way to go after all. Then, instead of no one wanting the wheelchair, it became a popular item. A lot of times, Danielle and Dominique shared the wheelchair together while Gabrielle walked and Nathanael rode in his stroller.

We also got to dine at several fine restaurants at no cost to us. We had what would have been a very expensive meal at the Hard Rock Cafe, but because of Danielle's button, it was free. At this restaurant, all of the kids received free t-shirts also. We also dined at a five-star Italian restaurant at the Epcot Center. However, Danielle's favorite was King Henry's Feast. This place was set in medieval times. We were pretending to celebrate the King's birthday. In the center stage, we watched fascinating entertainment such as juggling, a man swallowing a sword, a pretend fight between two knights and a trapeze artist.

Between courses of our meal, Philip was chosen to wear a bib and serve the food at our table. We were all wearing blue paper crowns. We all had a lot of fun! Danielle enjoyed the entertainment, the atmosphere, and especially laughing at her daddy.

At the end of the trip, Danielle stated the Magic Kingdom and King Henry's Feast were her favorites. She also loved the castle and carousel and the Give Kids the World Village. All of us were having such a good time. None of us were looking forward to our trip back home. We knew Danielle would have to face horrible suffering when we returned. It was so nice to live as a family having much fun for a week without any pain and suffering. The following week would be a whole different world.

The Bone Marrow Transplant

We arrived home from our trip on the evening of 7 December 1994. We came home briefly to pick up Danielle's suitcase, which was already packed for the hospital. Danielle was in a great mood after her wonderful trip. She also felt she was looking forward to the transplant, thinking it would be an experience that would save her life. She was told it would bring her immeasurable suffering, but it would also be something to kill her leukemia and save her life. If all ended successfully, the chemotherapy she hated would no longer be needed.

Once, Danielle stated she had already experienced all kinds of pain, so this pain would be nothing new to her. Unfortunately, she was wrong because it would be worse than she ever imagined. Like us, Danielle had prayed for the success of her transplant, and I feel she had a lot of faith in her prayers. We never told her there was a fifteen percent chance she could die, though I did read her books on dying, trying to prepare for what could happen.

During one of our hospital visits, while explaining to her there was a chance she may not survive the transplant, she stated, "Well, at least I won't have to come back to this place anymore." Death did not seem to scare her. As I have already stated, she had a great belief in a beautiful Heaven without pain and suffering and God's promise of eternity.

Before Danielle and I left for the hospital, she gave her sisters and brother a big kiss and a hug goodbye. Our eyes filled up with tears as Philip and I watched in sadness because, in the back of our minds, we were wondering if they would ever see Danielle alive again. We felt God would heal her, but we knew her death was a possibility. It was very difficult watching our children separated. They all loved each other so much! They enjoyed nothing more than just being together.

Our close family had to be torn apart. We all knew it would be a long time before our kids would be able to be with Danielle again. We were told Danielle might have to be in the hospital for thirty to ninety days, depending on how her body would react to the procedure. Children were not allowed to visit Danielle in her ICU room, for fear of Danielle contracting germs, though any adult who was considered well and had thoroughly washed hands was allowed in. The full-body radiation and massive doses of chemotherapy would cause her blood counts and immune system to plummet.

Unlike Danielle's regular hospital stays, she was given a room in the Intensive Care Unit. She was excited about her new and different room. Two of the walls were glass. Danielle felt it would be fun, but I felt like we were animals in a cage with people staring at us. The room was cold and solitary. There was very little privacy, sleeping was next to impossible.

After Danielle and I arrived in her room late after dark, we went to sleep only to be awakened at 4:30 a.m. to go down for Danielle's first radiation treatment. In a hospital, time on a clock is just a number. Danielle was never a morning person, and since she was exhausted from her big trip, this seemed like an impossible task to ask out of such a small child.

This is how the treatment began on 8 December, the Feast of the Immaculate Conception. My only consolation was knowing it was a beautiful Feast Day for Danielle to offer the beginnings of her horrible sufferings. The radiation was given while sitting up on a bicycle seat with her feet just barely touching the floor. The room was very cold. She had to take off her pajama shirt for the radiation technicians to set up. They had to take many X-rays and make sure her lungs were completely blocked from the radiation. It was very important that no radiation got into her lungs. If it did, that could lead to major problems.

I prayed for the angels to spread their wings and block Danielle's lungs from the radiation. After an X-ray was developed, the doctors were very excited. They were very proud of how well Danielle's lungs were blocked. They said it was rare to see such a perfect blockage. I felt happy and more at ease. I knew my prayer had been answered. It was not just the doctors who had done such a perfect job. It was accomplished by the assistance of God's heavenly angels. I have always felt angels are waiting to help, they just need to be asked.

Finally, after everything was all set up, it was time to begin. Danielle was told it was very important to sit as still as possible without any movement. I put in a tape cassette for her to listen to. I was hoping this would soothe her and keep her occupied for a while. I had to leave Danielle in the room by herself and watch her from the outside on a television monitor. I was also able to press a button on an intercom so Danielle could hear me. This first radiation treatment took almost two hours. She had to have these treatments twice daily, and fortunately, the remaining ones took less than an hour.

For the first three days of these radiation treatments, I had to sit and watch Danielle suffer miserably. I watched her on the monitor screen crying while trying to sit as still as possible on the bicycle seat. She was so tired and it was so boring for her. She cried out, "Mommy, Mommy, Mommy." I felt as though my heart was ripped apart, but what could I do?

I pressed the button on the intercom to communicate with her and said, "You're doing great, Danielle! Just keep holding still and it will all be over in a little bit." This never seemed to give her any comfort. I am sure the radiation treatments are easy for a lot of people, but for seven-year-old sleepyhead Danielle, they were quite a task. In fact, I would call it pure, agonizing torture. I had to sit and fight back my tears welling up in my eyes as I watched my child be so miserable.

The last two days of her radiation took place later in the morning. This helped things to go a lot easier for Danielle and she was able to endure them much better. Philip got to be with her for some of these treatments. We alternated days at the hospital with Danielle; therefore, we both got to spend time with her. This made it less stressful for us. It also gave us time to be with our other three children at home who needed us so desperately. They were suffering too in a different way.

Dominique, Gabrielle, and Nathanael all suffered during Danielle's hospital stays. They not only missed their beloved sister, they also missed having both a mother and a father together at home. We could usually see a significant change in all our children when Danielle was hospitalized. They argued more and seemed to be under more stress. Dominique and Gabrielle were upset about the idea of not being allowed in Danielle's room. It was just too difficult for them to comprehend. The only consolation they had was calling Danielle on the telephone to speak with her. There were, of course, no cell phones during that time.

Unfortunately, during the transplant, Danielle always felt too bad to talk with them. I think this made them worry even more about Danielle. They were very scared about what might be happening to their sister. We continually tried to console them by explaining Danielle was going to be okay and she would be home soon. It seemed like every day they would ask us how much longer Danielle would have to stay. Our children also had to get acquainted with a babysitter. Since Philip worked during the day and I had to stay at the hospital with Danielle, we had to find someone to take care of the children. Fortunately, a woman from church volunteered and she turned out to be very nice and helpful. It was still difficult for the children to adjust to different routines and a new person caring for them.

That first week in the hospital, Danielle felt really well. So far, we did not see any ill side effects from the radiation other than red eyes and a slight sunburn.

Danielle stayed busy doing crafts and painting the glass walls of her intensive care room. One wall she decorated with Christmas decorations. She painted a gingerbread house with gingerbread people and drew a clown. On the other wall, she painted Mickey Mouse and something special for her little brother, Nathanael. She drew a king without a face, just like the one she saw at Give Kids the World. She made it especially just for him so he could come and look at her through the glass wall. It worked perfectly because it was just his size. When he came to peek at her through the glass, he knew just what to do. When he looked through it, Danielle could see her beautifully-painted silly king with the face of her brother Nathanael. It always made her smile.

Immediately following the week of radiation treatments, Danielle was given massive doses of chemotherapy. The radiation and chemotherapy were used to kill all leukemia cells in her body. Unfortunately, at the same time, it destroys good blood cells used in the immune system. This makes the patient very susceptible to infection; therefore, anyone who entered Danielle's room had to wash and scrub their hands thoroughly. All nurses and visitors had to wear masks on their faces, but thankfully, Philip and I did not.

By the end of the radiation and chemotherapy, everything had begun to take its toll. It was time for Danielle to suffer as she never had before. Her problems began with severe vomiting every fifteen to twenty minutes around the clock. It seemed no medication brought her relief. Severe mouth sores covered her entire mouth and tongue, while blisters coated her throat.

Food became impossible for her to eat. Even swallowing water brought a grimace to her face. The only substance she would take by mouth would be small pieces of the Eucharist, and with time, this too became too painful. Her cheeks became swollen from the sores lining the inside of her mouth. She was given several mouthwashes to help numb the blisters, but they seemed to cause her a lot of pain and the relief they gave was so temporary. She was also given morphine for a little while, until it was decided she was allergic to it, since it caused her to itch severely. She was rarely able to get any sleep.

I prayed over her often and blessed her with the oil from the crying icon which Danielle loved, but nothing seemed to bring her relief. All our prayers could not take away her pain, but I believe they helped give her grace to endure her suffering. I once heard a priest say, "Suffering is a thermometer that measures the love of God in a soul." The doctors were amazed at how she rarely complained. Besides the radiation treatments, I only really heard her crying twice because of the pain.

Fr Henry Roberson came and gave the Sacrament of the Sick. He came on his own accord, as did many others. It really meant a lot to us to know people cared so much. Archbishop Eusibius Beltran was another special visitor. When he came to visit Danielle, she was sleeping, but he blessed her and visited with Philip for a moment. We always felt his love, care, and concern. He was truly a caring shepherd that loved his children. We were very happy he took the time to come and see her in the hospital, which meant a lot to us.

A parishioner from St. Andrew's came to visit Danielle. He brought a large picture of Jesus of Divine Mercy. At the bottom of the picture, it read, "Jesus, I Trust in You." This picture belonged to St. Andrew's Catholic Church and was kept under the tabernacle of their church. The parish allowed it to stay in Danielle's hospital room. Danielle loved having such a beautiful picture of Jesus right next to her hospital bed. I noticed she glanced at it often. The picture of Jesus not only gave Danielle comfort, but it also gave comfort to everyone who stayed in the room caring for her. Even some of the nurses noticed the picture and commented on how beautiful it was.

Now, when I see this picture or copies of a Divine Mercy picture, it reminds me of Jesus being with us all through those great times of suffering. The Divine Mercy has truly become a special devotion to me, but after Danielle's death, sometimes it brought tears to my eyes because it reminded me of her hospital room. Our family frequently prays the Divine Mercy Chaplet together and every Lent, we do a nine-day novena to the Divine Mercy of Jesus which ends on Divine Mercy Sunday. This devotion is very special and meaningful to our family.

It was incredible how many people were praying for Danielle! There was an all-night prayer vigil at St. Andrew's Catholic Church on 16 December 1994, when she received her transplant. We were amazed at the amount of people who went to the church before the Blessed Sacrament to pray for Danielle. The love and caring was overwhelming and much appreciated. This was the first forty-hour prayer vigil held at St. Andrew's Church.

As so many people were praying for Danielle, she received her new bone marrow from her generous donor. At the beginning, everything seemed to go smoothly. The bone marrow was given to her through her IV. There was no pain involved in the transplant. Along with the bone marrow, the donor sent Danielle a stuffed teddy bear and a beautiful card that said:

Dear Recipient,

My family and I send our love and warm wishes to you and your family. I feel very privileged to be of possible help to you. I hope your trip to Disney World was everything you hoped it would be and more.

Godspeed Little One,

Your Donor

A few days following the transplant, the vomiting continued to be so severe that the doctors tried some alternative nausea medication. So far nothing was giving her relief. Finally, the new medication began to help. The vomiting began to slow down to about six times a day. Just as she seemed to be doing better, though, the medication began having an ill effect on her. Danielle became listless.

When she was awake, she was unable to focus her eyes. Her eyes would roll back into her head and she lost control of her jaw muscles causing her to clench her teeth tight. She also had a high fever. It was very frightening. Even the nurse admitted she had never seen anything like it before. The nurse called the doctor and he asked for blood cultures to be drawn because of the fever. The doctor thought it was probably an allergic reaction and instructed the nurses to inject another type of medication into the catheter line which caused the bad reactions to stop very quickly and we were very relieved. Danielle said she was not afraid, but hated the feeling of losing control. She was braver than I was. I did not know what was happening to her. All of the blood cultures taken came back negative. In fact, there was never any sign of an infection during her entire hospital stay. Because of her negative response to the nausea medication, she had to stop taking it.

Things did not get any better. In fact, everything began taking a downward spiral. Danielle began to develop severe diarrhea from the radiation treatments. She was still very determined to get up and walk to the bathroom and refused to use a bedpan. I felt so bad for her. Once, I talked her into wearing an adult diaper to see if that would be any better. I didn't know who felt worse about this, me or her. I know Danielle felt so humiliated.

At the same time, it hurt me to see her so helpless. After this one time, she refused to wear any more of the diapers. At this time, I felt things could not possibly get worse. The combination of sores in her mouth, vomiting, constant nausea, diarrhea, high fevers and fatigue were so overwhelming. I felt so helpless and my heart was broken. The only way I could soothe my child was through continuous prayer. It was through prayer she was given so much peace, even though she felt so miserable.

Just as I was hoping and praying for a miracle of healing from the Infant Jesus, Danielle broke out in a severe body rash, including welts from head to toe on Christmas Day. She also began to itch severely and her body began to swell with a lot of extra fluid. Within a few days, she gained twelve pounds due to swelling. She began to look unrecognizable. Along with all this came very high fevers, once as high as one hundred and seven degrees. The nurses would remove all her blankets to try and reduce the fever. We watched helplessly as she shook with bodily chills.

We watched her live the last weeks of her life in total agony. All of her sufferings were offered to God in the hopes of saving many souls. I would stand over Danielle's bed and pray silently and out loud for her since she became too weak to think or speak much. She always trusted God and loved Him dearly. I think she always had hope that someday she would get better and return home to those she loved in her happy, secure little home. Instead, she would leave the hospital sooner than expected for her heavenly home—a true home full of joy, a place full of love, a place she would never have to suffer again.

Danielle's rash had become so severe that the doctors became very concerned. The doctor ordered for a dermatologist to come and cut out a piece of the rash so it could be examined more closely. Since Danielle had experienced having her skin scraped for the shingles test, I knew she would hate this even more. I had to explain to her what was going to happen, but I assured her they would try to make her very drowsy first with medication.

My mother came to be with Danielle and me to support us in this time of suffering. We waited and waited for the dermatologist. Danielle was very nervous and scared about what was going to happen.

When the cleaning lady came in to empty the trash, Danielle began crying thinking this was the doctor coming in to set up for the procedure. The nurses had given Danielle some morphine, but rather than put her to sleep, it caused her to itch even more. It was then I drew the conclusion the morphine was what was causing all of her horrible and unbearable itching.

Finally, the doctor arrived. Danielle began crying right away with great anxiety about what was going to happen. This dermatologist was a young man, most likely right out of college, and seemed very nervous about this task.

He worked in a private practice and stated he was not used to working on children in hospitals. He could tell Danielle was very scared and he appeared to dread the thought of hurting a child was obviously already in severe pain. He was also nervous about her moving during the procedure. Danielle was crying and asked me to hold her on my lap. The doctor decided to take a small piece of the rash from her thigh. Danielle was wide awake. She held very still, but cried the whole time. I was also crying quietly with silent tears streaming down my face. I hated seeing her suffer so much. I looked over at my mother across the room and she was crying too. Later, my mother told me she can hardly handle looking at a picture of the statue of Pieta (Mary holding Jesus in her arms after His death). She says the Pieta image reminded her so much of the way I was holding Danielle that day. It turned out to be the last day I would ever hold my little Danielle on my lap.

Danielle could not rest after the doctor was finished. He gave her a couple of stitches, then left to study the results. She was extremely exhausted, but couldn't sleep due to the severe itching caused by the morphine.

Later, the dermatologist returned to tell us he diagnosed Danielle with Graft versus Host Disease. This is a very unpleasant disease and is caused by the bone marrow transplant and can be fatal. After he left, my mother held me and we cried as we tried to accept the bad news. We had prayed so hard that she would not get this awful disease.

When I was able to speak with the bone marrow doctor, he told me he questioned the diagnosis. She had not yet shown her body was accepting the new bone marrow. Graft versus Host Disease can only be present when there is a graft, that is, when the blood counts start improving and the body shows its acceptance or unacceptance of its new marrow. The doctor said the test really told us nothing. Again, this seemed like such useless suffering for Danielle. The doctor stated, if her blood counts did not rise in the next two or three days, he would feel more definite this was not Graft versus Host.

Danielle died about five days later and she still showed no signs of accepting the bone marrow. It was expected to happen any day. The doctor felt the rash was due to a drug reaction and he was unsure which medication was the culprit. There was one particular drug, called Amphotericin B, Danielle had received as a prevention against fungal infection we thought was the culprit. In fact, Philip tried to persuade the doctor to take her off of it. We watched her grow worse each time it was given. Philip and I feel it was a drug that brought her to her death. After her death, we found out the nurses call this drug Amphoterrible, because if it didn't cure you, it would kill you. We will never know for sure, since we elected not to have an autopsy performed. We just could not see putting Danielle's body through more medical procedures when we already felt we knew, in our hearts, what caused her death. We also felt, if it was drug related or due to hospital error, they would never tell us the truth.

Going to Her Heavenly Home

Danielle was dying and we did not even know it. Even the doctors were fooled. They thought things were going well. She could barely see out of her eyes because the swelling was so severe. Her skin rash had become so horrible her face began to peel. The doctor warned us she might even blister. The vomiting slowed down a lot, but it became bloody. The diarrhea remained and the fevers relentlessly kept coming. When she had fevers, she always chilled uncontrollably. One time, Philip said he tried to help by covering her with his body and she shook him also. The nurses had to remove all her covers to help bring the fevers down. I know Danielle hated this, as she begged to keep at least the sheet on. Every little bit of comfort was being ripped away from her. It was hard not to beat ourselves up, wondering why we chose this path or misery.

On Saturday, 31 December 1994, I brought our other children up to the hospital to see Danielle through the glass wall of her room. They stared at her, as they saw her looking miserable, lying in agony. It was so painful for her sisters to see her this way. They all wanted to hug and touch her so badly. Dominique was very concerned about the visible swelling and skin rash. Danielle's feet were a purplish color and her toes were very brown. I think this frightened Dominique greatly.

Since Danielle could barely tolerate sitting up, they moved around to the other glass wall which faced the side of her bed. They smiled and waved at her. As I begged her to say hello, she weakly raised her hand and waved back. She also managed to put a small smile on her face. It was the first time, we had seen Danielle smile in the past few days. It was obvious to see the love she had for them. It caused my heart to break when I thought of how badly they wanted to touch each other. I think a touch from them could have given her so much comfort. She never got to touch them one last time. This separation with her siblings, I believe, was probably her greatest suffering of all.

Later that day, Danielle asked her daddy to bless her again with the oil from her special crying icon. Just as Mary was united with Jesus' suffering, Danielle united her sufferings with theirs. I feel Danielle had an incredibly mature understanding of the sufferings of Jesus and Mary, which was a love and maturity way beyond what most adults will ever feel or comprehend. Even through her tremendous suffering, she always loved God and continued to have great faith.

Looking back in time, I believe God accepted my total offering of Danielle, when I was pregnant with her and consecrated her to Him. I did this again after she was born. My only real desire for her was to be very pleasing to God and bring many souls to Him. My most important goal for all of my children has always been the eternal reward of Heaven. I have never had regrets about my offering of Danielle or any of my children. Danielle was a gift to Jesus and I feel, through her sufferings, she helped save many souls who needed her offerings and prayers. Without her sweet and innocent sufferings, many souls probably would have been lost. She must now be in total and complete joy, being able to see all the beautiful souls she caused to radiate by her burning offering of loving and innocent sufferings.

On Sunday, 1 January 1995, the Solemnity of Mary, Mother of God, we all woke up to what we thought would be just another day. Philip was with Danielle at the hospital all day. I went to Sunday morning mass with our other children. Afterward, the kids and I went to Philip's parents' house for lunch, just as we did on many Sundays. It was important to keep our lives as normal as possible for the sake of the kids. We all had absolutely no idea how severe Daneielle's condition was getting, since the doctors believed things were going well. That afternoon, I called my niece, Sondra, to babysit so I could be with Danielle and Philip at the hospital. I was blessed to be able to go visit there for a couple of hours. As usual, Danielle was suffering miserably. She had developed a dry cough which was very bothersome to her.

Now we know this cough was the beginning of congestive heart failure. She complained a lot more than usual about her throat hurting. She was very weak, but agreed to take a bath for me. She only stayed in the tub, which was really just a rubber storage container, for a very short time because the pain was too intense to sit up for any period of time. When it was time for her to stand up, she cried and said she couldn't. I could tell then she was really growing weak. She got out of the tub and was moaning with pain and exhaustion. I wrapped her in a clean cotton blanket to dry her off. I then held her in my arms for a short time and kissed her, telling her I loved her very much. She was much too weak to respond with any affection in return. I helped her get dressed and put her into bed, covering her with a Disney Snow White blanket she had received as a Christmas present from her great aunt, Tia Margarita. Danielle was very proud of her special blanket.

Danielle continued to cough and spray numbing spray into her throat. She could not settle down to rest because the cough had become so severe. She had been given cough suppressants, but nothing was helping her. She still had diarrhea and was vomiting blood, along with her horribly whelped skin rash and fevers.

It seemed she was hardly ever able to get much sleep; just another cross she carried. I read to her a copy of a Christmas letter by Pope John Paul II to Children in the year of the family. The letter was dated 13 December 1994. The last words of the letter read, "Raise your tiny hand, Divine child and bless these young friends of yours, bless the children of all the earth." After reading the letter, I tried to continue to soothe her and played quiet, peaceful music. It was getting late, so I kissed her goodbye for the very last time. If only I would have known she was going to die that night, I would have never left her bedside. Though difficult, I do believe as Danielle's dream foretold, it was meant for her to be alone with her daddy on her last night of her earthly life.

I hugged and kissed Philip goodbye also. I missed him so much! I hated leaving them, especially with Danielle suffering so horribly.

After I left the hospital, Danielle continued to struggle with sleeping. Philip did not know what to do for her. Being a doctor, he was used to helping people get better, but now he was helpless. He started to become frustrated because he thought, *If Danielle could fall asleep, she would feel much better.* She tried to stop coughing, but could not. The only thing he could do, which helped a little, was to rub her back. This good stimuli seemed to calm her. It only lasted a short time though, because the nurses came into the room, so he went back to his bed, not being in the way.

Philip was trying to keep his sanity by painting a picture and watching a football game. But the more he tried to cope, the more Danielle seemed to need him. Not only was she coughing constantly, but she had frequent urges to have to go to the bathroom and needed assistance unplugging her IV pole and carrying her to the bathroom. Each time he took her, she said she could not go. After several attempts, Philip was getting even more frustrated. It was so hard for him to see her feeling so bad and not be able to do anything to help her.

Later in the evening, about 9:30 to 10:00 p.m., Philip called me from the hospital and said Danielle was coughing a lot. He told me about all the trips to the bathroom and how he could do nothing to help. Philip said the nurse had come and taken blood from Danielle's arm, but she only cried a little. She was too weak to put up a fight or complain. I reassured Philip, telling him things would be okay. I told him to talk soothingly to Danielle and to continue rubbing her back. I reminded him she was in intense suffering and needed extra love and attention.

He was also very tired since he had been at the hospital for the last few nights and it was impossible to get rest there. Danielle was always hurting and there were always so many distractions for sleep. When I hung up from the phone call, Philip seemed to be more settled. It was so hard for me not to be there with her when she needed me so much.

About 11:00 p.m. Philip called me again, after taking Danielle to the bathroom once again. This time he was scared. He stated he did not think Danielle was going to make it. I asked him what he meant. He told me he had never seen her look or feel so bad. He explained to me how she was continuing to grow weaker. When she returned to the bed, she fell onto her side with her arms in a very uncomfortable position. She had no strength to move them. This was the first time Philip actually felt Danielle might die, but he had not relayed that feeling to me. To that point, he knew Danielle was very bad, but he always thought she would recover. I told him that I would come up and be with them if he wanted me to. I really wanted to go, and I definitely would have if I had any idea she was dying. I felt she was going to be okay and I also had the other kids to consider. He said he thought he was probably just over-reacting, and if they got through that night, everything would be okay. I asked him again if he was sure. I told him I could find a babysitter for our other kids, even though it was late and our kids were already asleep.

Again, he said, "No, things would be fine." I then asked for him to please call me if things got any worse. After I got off the phone, I took a shower, crying the whole time, thinking about Danielle and praying for her. I was very upset and frightened. I knelt before our picture of the Sacred

Heart of Jesus and prayed and cried, begging for God's help for Danielle and peace for us all.

Danielle had to go to the bathroom once again, so Philip unplugged her IV pole and said, "Let's go." She tried, but had no strength to move. Philip was very scared and started to cry.

He told her, "Please, Danielle, try, try!" He got her around the waist and carried her to the bathroom. Her body was limp. Her head just laid on his shoulder, and her arms and legs dangled. She kept saying, "Dad…dy." Philip will never forget her cry for help. When Philip got her into the bathroom, he said she was lifeless. He had to grab a handful of her shirt so she would not fall over. She said, "Daddy, I can't." Philip asked her, or begged her, to try to walk back to her bed.

He did not want her to quit trying. He knew Danielle was a fighter and did not want to quit, so he was encouraging her. She stood up, then collapsed onto his shoulder. After getting on her feet, again she took a few more steps, but they were very uncoordinated and unstable.

He grabbed hold of her and got her back to her bed. After collapsing, he asked her if she was okay. She nodded, 'yes'. Then, he asked her if she was scared and she nodded, 'no'. To me, this reaffirmed she was not afraid of dying. Philip also told me, in that same moment, she was staring at the upper corner of the room for a period of time, which made him wonder if she was seeing a heavenly vision. This could possibly have been part of her beautiful dream she had when she and her daddy were alone and she heard the angels singing. It also reminded me of the times when she was a toddler and would stare at the corner of the room when we thought she could be seeing her guardian angel.

The nurses came in to hook up monitors to Danielle. Philip was very scared and decided to call me again. As the phone was ringing, Philip watched as Danielle rolled to her stomach and lifted her bottom up two times, kind of high as if she was struggling for air. At that exact time, I picked up the phone. In a rushed voice that was breaking up, he said, "Myra, I think you better get up here right away! Danielle's dying!"

I said, "Okay, I'll be there as soon as possible!" I could hear a lot of commotion in the background, but I did not know what was happening. Later, Philip told me it was the nurse shouting, "Danielle! Danielle! Code Blue!" The nurse turned Danielle over onto her back, but Danielle's body was limp. Philip feels at this time she was already dead. It was approximately 11:34 p.m. The nurses did CPR and injected different medications, trying to revive her to no avail. They declared Danielle dead on 2 January 1995, at 12:02 a.m. Later, I learned 2 January was the birthday of Danielle's favorite saint, St. Therese of Lisieux. I feel it was very special Danielle not only died on 1 January, the Solemnity of the Mother of God, but she was also able to enter Heaven on her patron saint's birthday.

When I got off the phone with Philip, my whole body was trembling. All I could say was, "Oh, God. Please, God help her!" I then had to think quickly of someone to watch my kids. I called my brother, Matt. He lived very close and could be at my house in a short time. Matt showed up within ten minutes with his daughter, Kathryn. I ran outside to meet them. I was crying frantically.

Kathryn went into the house to watch the kids and Matt wrapped his arm around my waist and helped me to his car. He told me he would drive because he knew I was very upset and scared. Matt said things would be alright and Danielle would be fine. He tried to comfort me while at the same time driving very fast to get to the hospital. When we arrived, all the main doors were locked, but I knew the emergency room doors would be open. So, we quickly ran to the back of the hospital through the emergency room doors, looking for the nearest elevator. Another man stepped onto the elevator with us. Little did we know he was a chaplain who was also on his way to Danielle's room.

Both Matt and I got on the elevator and silently went to Danielle's floor, breathing heavily. After exiting the elevator, I came around the corner to where Danielle's room was and saw her glass door wide open with the bright lights on. My heart was racing as I was storming Heaven with prayers. I couldn't get there fast enough! Philip and the doctor were standing in the hall along with several nurses.

I knew immediately she must have died. It was like the energy in my body left me. I dropped my purse and dropped to my knees. I began wailing like a baby. I was crying out, "My beautiful baby girl!" I was so shocked and upset. Philip helped me up and held me calmly in his arms as I continued to cry.

He just kept saying, "Myra, I'm sorry. I'm so sorry." He felt so bad for me. I cried and stomped my feet. I was sad and angry at the same time. I was mad because the doctors had assured me she was doing fine. I was also angry because I did not get to be with her when she took her last breath. I thought to myself, *How could this be happening?* It was like a really bad dream, but I knew it was real. It was very real!

When I regained some strength, I walked over to look at Danielle lying in her bed with the Snow White blanket covering her little body I had tucked her in with earlier. I could hardly stand to look at her. She had a long, bloody tube in her mouth had been used in the attempt to resuscitate her. Philip said he did not think she felt any pain. He believed she died immediately with her last breath before the nurse turned her over on her back. This gave me some relief. I could not bear the thought of her suffering anymore.

When we decided not to have an autopsy, the tube was removed from her throat. Her face looked very peaceful. It was the best I had seen her in over a month. The day before she died, the rash and swelling on her head and face had mysteriously began to disappear, while the rest of her body was still covered and swollen. I feel God was preparing her body to be viewed for her death.

A little later, Danielle's grandparents arrived at the hospital and all of them were in tears. The last they had heard was Danielle was doing fine. Thankfully, after Philip hung up the phone with me earlier, he called Fr John McMenamin, the associate pastor at St. James. Father showed up shortly after our parents. He anointed Danielle's body and we all gathered together and prayed.

Danielle's hematology doctor came and was very kind. He had nothing to do with the bone marrow transplant, but he had come to check on Danielle several times while she was being hospitalized. He hugged us and told us he was very sorry. It was obvious he felt bad for us. He said he would always remember Danielle. I gave him a picture of her to make sure he would never forget. He stayed and helped us pack up all our belongings. Everything had to be cleaned out that very night. It was such a nightmare and a memory and I will never forget.

Our Loss Is His Gain

Philip and I left the hospital together and went home to be with our other children. The pain we felt from the loss of our beloved Danielle was beyond what I can describe. Our five-year-old daughter, Gabrielle, woke up when we got home, so we decided to tell her Danielle had died. She first started to smile because I think she was confused, then she began to cry. We held her and comforted her. We reminded her of the peace and happiness Danielle was now experiencing in Heaven with all the angels and saints. I feel because of all Danielle's sufferings, and our own suffering, God had showered our family with His great love and beautiful graces that gave us the extra strength and hope we needed to still remain peaceful and hopeful in a catastrophic time for our family.

Danielle's death brought us great sadness, but did not cause us depression. We are sad because we miss Danielle, but at the same time we are happy she is in a far better place, united with Jesus. Her pain and earthly sufferings have ended. We have accepted God's will and trust in His plan. The Holy Spirit has continued to give us comfort and peace. Without God and our strong Catholic faith, peace and happiness would not be possible for us.

The next morning, Philip and I got up from bed very early, since sleeping was next to impossible. We had the dreadful job of making arrangements for Danielle's funeral and her internment. Before we left for the funeral home, I had the awful task of collecting Danielle's belongings to be worn for her burial. I decided she would wear her burgundy, velvet dress. It was a dress she had chosen herself and bought with her birthday money from her great aunt Barbara. When she bought this beautiful dress, she thought she would be wearing it for Christmas.

We had thought her bone marrow transplant would probably be scheduled after Christmas. Instead, it took place right during the Holy season. When she brought the dress home from the store, I privately told Philip I felt she would either be wearing that dress for Christmas or she would be buried in it. The dress also had a beautiful, velvet hat to match, with a cream-colored silk rose on the front brim. Under the hat, she would wear her white, silk scarf. I also gathered a little brown scapular, her pin of St. Therese and a Miraculous Medal. I then found a pair of her white tights and her black patent dress shoes. She was going to look very beautiful. The only other time she was able to wear the dress was at her photo shoot taken by Glamour Shots which is still hanging in our home today.

My parents and a friend of the family, Barbara, came that morning to help us make arrangements about the funeral, obituary, and mass. Before we left, we decided to wake Dominique to share with her the painful news of her big sister's death. We felt it was important for us to be the ones to tell her. I told Dominique, "Last night, Danielle, went to Heaven to be with Jesus." She knew immediately what that meant, and looked at both of us and began to cry. I held her tightly and assured her everything would be okay and God would take care of us. I explained to her Danielle was with Jesus now and her suffering was over.

Dominique was very upset and rightfully so. She said repeatedly, "You told me she was going to come home!" Many years later, she would still remind us of the unkept promise. We had always told the girls that Danielle would eventually get better and come home to be with us again. My heart broke for them and continued breaking in so many ways. Dominique was only fifteen months younger than Danielle. They were best friends and did everything together, spending every moment of the day side by side. I believe it was Dominique who most likely suffered the most from this unexpected death. I used to tell Danielle and all my children, if we offer up our sufferings, Mary would give a rose to Jesus. After Danielle's death, Dominique stated, "Now, Jesus is covered with roses because Danielle suffered so much." I feel sure she is right.

Next, we had to explain Danielle's death to two-year-old Nathanael. I said, "Sissy Danielle went to be with Jesus. She went Bye-Bye." I also told him, "She is in Heaven now." Nathanael knew who Jesus was and I felt, within a few days, he was really able to somewhat grasp and understand what was happening. Nathanael was only two years old at the time, but he seemed to have a remarkable understanding and awareness of his faith and the spiritual world for his age. One morning, it seemed all he chatted about was Jesus, Mary and the angels. Danielle was so very close to her little brother and I'm certain she still continues to look out for him and pray for him, as she does for all her siblings.

After the kids were told about their sister's death, we left them with my mother, Jan, and our friend Barbara. Barbara was a great support for my mother who was also suffering so much. Philip and I had to take care of business at the funeral home and cemetery. My father, John, went along with us for support and advice. We, fortunately, had never dealt so closely with a death and were not sure how to handle things. I knew this was very difficult for my father because he was also very close to Danielle and we were still all in such shock. All our sufferings were crying out to the Lord, but He was giving us the graces we needed to help us through and carry our cross.

Finally, after a very long, difficult morning, we returned home. We were so tired and felt as though we were sleepwalking through a bad dream. Our house was full of caring people when we returned. Everyone was so kind, offering their prayers, support and an abundance of God's love. God wanted to make sure we were well taken care of. We wanted this support, but at this same time, we wanted time to grieve alone. Philip and I decided to go back into our bedroom and shut the door for a while. We laid on the bed, held each other and cried. Then, our children came in and joined us.

Dominique and Gabrielle also clung to us and cried, especially Dominique. She seemed to be having the hardest time. There was a yellow balloon Dominique chose as the place to express her feelings. On it, she wrote a message for Danielle. The balloon read, "I love you, Danielle! I miss you! What do angels look like? You're a Saint, Danielle."

Dominique also composed a song called, "You Are a Saint, Danielle." Drawing, writing and singing became a way for the girls to release their emotional feelings about their sister's death.

Later, we took the kids to view Danielle's body at the funeral home. This was really the first time they had ever experienced seeing a dead body. We were not sure how they would respond, but we felt it was important for them to see Danielle one last time. We also thought it would help them understand she was no longer in her body and she was in Heaven.

When we first entered Danielle's room at the funeral home, Nathanael began to smile. He was happy to see his big sister, thinking she was only sleeping. I touched Danielle, showing them not to be afraid. They also touched her, feeling the coldness of her once-warm face. Gabrielle talked about how Danielle had a new, different kind of body now. She said Danielle would be glad she doesn't have her old body anymore and she was very right. Danielle's body showed all the signs of pain and suffering, such as, no hair, no eyelashes, no eyebrows, horrible swelling made her look heavy and an ugly skin rash covering her body. Danielle's body did not look anything like all the memories we had of her and the beautiful way we each remembered her.

No pictures were taken of her in the casket because I didn't want to remember her in this horrible way. When we left the funeral home, Dominique and Gabrielle cried and I think Nathanael was beginning to understand. As a whole, it appeared as if they were handling the situation very well, but I know the wounds were deep.

Preparing for Her Union
With Christ

After visiting Danielle's body at the funeral home, we went home and tried to prepare ourselves for the Rosary Wake Service would take place the next day. We also worked on helping make some of the decisions about the funeral mass. I am so thankful our family had so many wonderful friends. They helped prepare the Rosary Wake Service and the funeral mass that both turned out to be very beautiful.

The evening of 3 January 1995, we left to go to the Rosary Wake Service for Danielle. On the way to the Rosary, little Nathanael pointed up out the window of the car. He was pointing and saying, "Danielle, Jesus, Angels, up there!" Mysteriously, no one ever told Nathanael Heaven was up. After that incident, he always pointed up when speaking of Heaven. Later, when we mentioned Danielle to him, he would point up and say, "Danielle in Heaven with Jesus." He would also say, "St. Bernadette up there," or "St. Therese in Heaven." When he saw a picture of any saint he recognized, he always said, "Up in Heaven with Jesus." I still wonder if Nathanael really did see Danielle in a heavenly vision on the car ride that evening. Maybe it was God comforting him, showing him his big sister was happy in her new home. Regardless of whether Nathanael saw something miraculous or imagined it, I do believe Nathanael was given great grace from the Holy Spirit to understand and accept his big sister's death so beautifully.

We reached St. James Catholic Church with a feeling of peace. God had allowed Nathanael to ease our minds a little that evening. God also helped us all understand just a little piece of joy Danielle was then experiencing. We chose St. James Church for the Rosary Wake Service rather than the funeral home because we felt the prayers are much more powerful in a church, in front of Jesus in the Blessed Sacrament.

Once inside the church, Philip and I met with our good friend, Fr Lee Kaylor, to help him plan how the rosary would be recited. It was determined Fr Kaylor would officiate the rosary while other friends and family would help lead the mysteries. The instrumental music was beautifully played by pianist Steve Seeds. We had met him at a benefit concert he organized and performed for Danielle's medical fund. He was very nice and had been very generous, loaning his outstanding talent to our family. After Danielle's death, he founded the Angel Wings Foundation, which helps provide financial assistance for families most in need through benefit concerts, fund-raising events, and cash donations.

The church was full of many people. Everything turned out to be very beautiful, as planned. It was very difficult seeing Danielle's swollen body, especially because she did not look like herself at all. The funeral home was able to cover her body rash with makeup, but her eyelashes and eyebrows were missing. Though seeing Danielle was difficult and we were exhausted, we managed to stay peaceful and calm. We cried, but it seemed Philip and I spent more time comforting other people rather than them comforting us. The Holy Spirit had given us tremendous strength through all the prayers that were holding us up.

The next day, 4 January 1995, Danielle had her funeral mass at St. James Catholic Church. Coincidentally, this is the same date of the baptism of St. Therese. The church was overflowing with many people. Some even had to sit in the church balcony because there was no room left in the sanctuary of the church. Fr Kastner, our parish priest, seemed very surprised to see such a large crowd. He said it was the second-largest funeral mass he had known of in all his years as pastor of St. James Parish. Danielle was very much loved.

My three brothers, Matt, Brian, and Greg, placed the Pall over Danielle's casket before the casket was brought down the aisle. Philip's brothers, John, Joe, Dan, Mike, Luis and Tomas were the Pallbearers. We entered the church as a large family. Philip, our kids, and I sat in the front row. Fr Kastner was the main celebrant and Fr Henry Roberson gave a beautiful homily. Many other priests and deacons who were friends of our families were also present. Altogether, there were nine priests and two deacons on the altar. Archbishop Beltran told us he would have tried to make it, but he was out of town at the time.

Since we were still in the Christmas season, the church was still beautifully decorated with the manger scene, poinsettias, and lighted Christmas decorations. All the Christmas lights on the altar added to this glorious funeral mass. The music was provided by the Crim family, along with a little girl from St. James School. She beautifully sang, 'Away in the Manger'. I am sure Danielle was overjoyed with such a beautiful mass and all the love that was present. Our friend, Barbara, read a eulogy after the mass and another good friend of the family, Ruth, read a beautiful poem she wrote for me. So many people commented it was the most beautiful funeral mass they had ever witnessed.

I was very saddened about losing Danielle, but at the same time, I was enraptured by the magnificent mass that brought me a sense of peace and a great feeling of love and hope. It helped me even more to deal with Danielle's death and realize how truly happy she must be.

After the funeral, we went to Resthaven Cemetery, in South Oklahoma City, where Danielle was laid to rest in the Garden of Hope. We chose this cemetery because it was close to our home and we have many relatives buried there. As an added blessing, we were able to purchase cemetery plots close to the statue of the Resurrected Jesus. When I visit Danielle's grave, the statue of Jesus always reminds me, like Him, we will all be resurrected in a glorious body on the last day.

At the grave site, the service continued to be very touching and beautiful. A song for Danielle was played on a cassette tape. It was a song we tried to play at her birthday mass, but at that time it would not play. On her birthday, we were disappointed because it did not play, but we felt there was a reason. Now, we know why. The name of the song was, 'Come Little Child', from the Album *Say Yes,* by the Catholic Irish singer, Dana. As the song played, everyone present was given a little bottle of bubbles to blow. The bottle read, "I carry this to remind me how fragile my spirit can become, but with one BREATH abundant joy can be mine." Everyone blew these bubbles for Danielle. It was as if Nathanael understood what it was all about. He smiled and blew his bubbles right toward Danielle's casket, which was covered by a beautiful blanket of pink flowers. I cried and smiled at the same time as I watched Nathanael and his sisters show this one last gesture of love for their big sister, Danielle.

After we left the cemetery, we went back to St. James Church for a funeral dinner. All the family seemed to be doing fine. Almost everyone we knew was very supportive and concerned about our wellbeing. About two hundred sympathy cards flooded into our home over the next few weeks. Several women from the parish and also friends and family cooked meals for us for about two weeks following Danielle's death. This was very generous and helpful. I wish everyone could experience this kind of love and generosity after the death of a loved one. It makes the pain a little easier to bear. Through all of the outreach and love of others, I learned a wonderful lesson in charity and loving my neighbor.

Death Is Not the End

There is no way for me to explain the painful heartache I have felt in the death of my first child. The agony of a parent, at the loss of a child, is far too great and overwhelming for another person to fully comprehend. At the same time, it is also hard to describe the joy we still have because of the many graces we have been blessed with by God. These beautiful graces from God have been gifted to us and have helped us accept Danielle's death as a perfect offering to Him. I believe it has been through our acceptance and embracing the cross of our sufferings we have been given these graces.

Danielle suffered so much and showed acceptance for her sufferings with peace and total love for God. Since she was newly confirmed and had received the Sacrament of the Sick and the Eucharist, she was in a beautiful state of grace.

These Sacraments caused her soul to overflow with God's grace, and at the moment of her death, those graces were overflowing upon her family to give us the strength to endure our new sufferings with love and acceptance.

I agree totally with something St. Elizabeth Ann Seton once said upon the death of one of her children. She said, "It would be too selfish in us to have wished her inexpressible sufferings prolonged and her secure bliss deferred for our longer possession…though in her I have lost the little friend of my heart." Another beautiful quote that has comforted me is, "The good God does not need years to accomplish His work of love in a soul: One ray from His heart can, in an instant, make His flower bloom for eternity." This quote was from Danielle's favorite saint, St. Therese of Lisieux and was printed on the back of the holy cards distributed at Danielle's funeral mass.

Enduring the agony of Danielle's suffering and death has brought me much closer to the pain and suffering of Our Lord and His Blessed Mother. Now, as never before in my life, the Stations of the Cross and the Sorrowful Rosary Mysteries come more alive for me and have led me to deeper spiritual meditations and prayer life. The statue of the Pieta has become one of my favorite images. I find it easier to understand and unite with the sufferings of the Blessed Mother. I believe Our Lady of Sorrows understands my sufferings and has great sympathy for me as a mother and prays for me.

Once, while at mass, Jesus gave me a beautiful enlightenment on suffering. When Jesus suffered and died, His cup was overflowing. My sufferings with Danielle were only a small taste of what Jesus and His Mother suffered. I had the feeling Jesus was agreeing with me at the moment I drank from the chalice of the Precious Blood. As a sign of understanding, I noticed there was only one very small drop left in the chalice. After taking this small, precious sip, I realized Jesus was saying to me, "Yes, your sufferings are only a very small taste of mine and my Mother's on Calvary at the crucifixion, but still very precious."

Another thought that has given me comfort through my sorrow and grief is knowing Danielle died at the age of seven. I once heard a priest say, "Seven is the signature of the Holy Spirit." According to the Bible, seven has been said to be a perfect number. I also believe it is beautiful she died in her innocence. Danielle had no idea how much evil lives and prowls in the world. She never had to be exposed to all the evil and sin would have surrounded and tested her later in life. The young innocence she had was spared and her purity was a gift to God.

It is my belief God accomplished good works in Danielle. While she was not perfect, she lived her life for Him and served Him the best way she knew how. She offered her sufferings for the sins of others. I feel she even gave her life for them. The thought in my heart has been believing Jesus and Mary accepted her sufferings with loving, open arms. I have never felt God caused Danielle's sufferings, but I do believe He saw her soul was willing to suffer, so He allowed these sufferings. Since her soul was so generous and willing to help others, there was no prayer or miracle that could take away her suffering or prevent her death. All the prayers said for Danielle were answered—not in a way we expected, but they were answered.

. The prayers lifted us up and gave us peace and strength during the midst of turmoil. The prayers also gave us so many blessings and graces. Danielle was very touched by all the people who prayed for her. I am sure she continues to pray for all of these people who had reached out to her in prayer. Even many years later, our family continues to benefit from all the prayers and the graces we have received from our acceptance Danielle is in the arms of God.

When Danielle was first diagnosed with leukemia, I wondered if it was an attack by the devil since she was such a good child and loved God so much. Maybe this belief was true, but if so, God was the real victor. The devil would have enjoyed nothing more than for Danielle and all of our family to lose our faith, but instead it backfired. Her illness not only brought more faith and love of God into the hearts of our family, it has affected our friends and even strangers all over the country who had been praying for her. By our continuing acceptance of Danielle's death as a love offering to God, I believe the Devil is still being defeated and graces are still being poured out upon us.

I want to share, Danielle had mentioned her desire to become a nun on several occasions. I believe she wanted nothing more than to serve God and help others. If she would have lived and grown up to do this, I am sure she would have helped some souls, but she could not have possibly helped and had the impact on as many people as she has with all her suffering and her death. She accomplished something so much greater in less amount of time. She already lived her vocation of love, service and devotion. She accomplished the goal the Lord set before her and the same goal is the one we are all reaching for, Heaven.

Sadly, so many people believe our goal here on earth is to be beautiful, educated, rich, famous, and other secular priorities. So many souls live for this earthly world and that is exactly what Satan wants. So many times, it is easy to get too attached to and absorbed with people around us, even over-attachment to family members. Many do not realize the only pleasure we need to seek is God's love and He, above everyone, must come first in our lives. We must live to know Him, serve Him, and love Him to the best of our human ability. We are all called to be Saints. Our life on earth determines where our souls will spend eternity. We all have to ask ourselves, "Are we living our lives as disciples of Christ? Or are we living them for our own self love?" Maybe then, we will be wishing we died young, in our innocence, before the world had a chance to corrupt our souls.

Looking at things in this perspective, we can no longer look at Danielle with pity, but with envy to see the soul that was taken in its innocence, adorned with love for God. Just as the Bible teaches us in Mark 10: 14–15, "Let the children come to me and do not hinder them. It is to just such as these that the kingdom of God belongs. I assure you that whoever does not accept the reign of God like a little child shall not take part in it. The Bible also says, in Romans 8: 16–17, The Spirit himself gives witness with our spirit that we are children of God. But if we are children, we are heirs as well; heirs of God, heirs with Christ, if only we suffer with Him so as to be glorified with Him." I will end Danielle's story with a correct perspective on life by St. John Paul II, "There is an urgent need to recover a correct perspective on life as a whole. The correct perspective is that of eternity, for which life at every phase is a meaningful preparation."

Thoughts From Dad

Danielle had a short, beautiful life as Myra described, but it was her death that actually deepened my faith. In fact, I credit Danielle for the conversion of my soul. I do realize Christ is the only true salvation, but Danielle's sufferings brought it more to life for me. I have seen miracles, such as rosaries turning different colors, and images in pictures, and even what appeared to be the sun dancing, but none of these touched my soul to completely give my life to God, to prioritize Him. Those were moments of fascination rather than conversion experiences. For some people, that would be enough, but for whatever reason, it took the loss of my daughter for me to turn toward God and grow in my love for Him.

I have had several events in my life where it felt like I was close to God. One such experience was Cursillo. Cursillo is a weekend retreat that has one totally focused on Christ and one's relationship with Him through listening to talks, building friendships, praying, mass, and adoration. Unfortunately, for me, though, as my life became more concerned with worldly things, I would lose my focus and drift away. Now, with Danielle's death, it is as if Danielle is taking me by the hand and every time I start to fall, she encourages and pushes me as I tried to do for her on her last day. The feeling of Christ's presence I once had through the experience of Cursillo is back, but this time, it is forever present during the trials and tribulations of life because my daughter will not allow me to fall back.

The night Danielle died, I was very upset because I felt I was alone with Danielle. I was very stressed, frustrated, tired, etc. I needed support, while at the same time needing to give support and comfort. Then Danielle took her last breaths. I needed a different type of support. The support I was given was the image of the Divine Mercy that was in Danielle's room. As the doctors and nurses were trying to revive Danielle, I went over to the nightstand the picture was propped up on. I was in shock and totally collapsed. It was as if all my energy was taken from my body. When I was regaining my strength, I pushed myself up using the nightstand. The first thing I saw was the picture of Jesus and the words, 'Jesus, I Trust in You'. At the time, the first thought was God would allow Danielle's life to continue and she would be miraculously revived.

Now, I have come to realize the trust I needed was to trust in Him with death as I did with all the new lives He entrusted to Myra and me when we did not think we could handle them.

I have heard of many people becoming upset with God or doubting the existence of God when in a similar situation. With all the prayers being said, by not just Catholics, but all denominations across the country, you would have thought Danielle should have been healed. I do feel she was cured, not in a physical sense, but in the most perfect way possible—being, going to Heaven. And, by her heavenly healing, she will be able to help heal my soul so I may one day join her to worship God for eternity. Her life and death has reaffirmed the existence of God and Heaven for me. This is the worst thing I have ever experienced, but at the same time, it is the best thing that has happened to me. Don't get me wrong. I would not wish this on anyone, but I am grateful it was allowed to happen to me. The feeling of God's love, grace, and peace has never felt stronger.

I have learned you must accept God's will, regardless of how the outcome appears. I was very frustrated the night of her death because I was not in control and I could not do anything to comfort her. I wanted to protect my child, but felt helpless. What I needed was an understanding of what was actually happening at that moment. Now, since I have had time to reflect on it, I feel God was asking Danielle if she was ready to join Him, and she accepted. His will was to have her in closer union with Him, while at the same time He knew this experience would increase my desire to please Him.

Every day I think of Danielle—the good times and the bad times. And every day, I am saddened by my loss, but by the same token, I thank God her death has affected my life in a way that leads me closer to Him.

Since her death, I have read several books on the lives of various saints. It seems the main theme of all their lives was to totally abandon themselves and turn their lives completely to God. In a sense, in order to live, you have to die to yourself. Danielle did this. For example, Danielle often said she was glad she had leukemia rather than her sisters or brother. To place them above herself is remarkable to me, especially for someone of her age. So, for me, Danielle is and always will be my little saint.

Epilogue

After Danielle's death, we had accumulated over $130,000.00 in hospital and doctor bills. We had only $25,000.00 remaining in the Danielle Martinez Fund. Since we knew there was no way we could pay the entire medical bill, we offered the hospital the remaining amount in Danielle's fund as our last payment on her bill. The hospital generously accepted and dismissed the difference of the entire bill. We were extremely thankful!

After the bill was paid, we had collected $2,500.00 and it was used to purchase a beautiful life-size statue of the Blessed Mother. There is a memorial plaque with Danielle's picture at the base of this statue. This, Our Lady of Grace statue, is a replica of one in Medjugorje at the church of St. James the Greater, where the Blessed Mother has been said to appear to visionaries. Our statue spent many years at Immaculate Conception Church in Oklahoma City, but now has a home at the John Paul II Dwelling where I volunteer at a home for those dying.

The statue was delivered to the home on 17 September, which was Danielle's birthday, also the same day the John Paul II Dwelling was purchased by the Gospel of Life Disciples. Besides God calling me to volunteer and minister there, Danielle's godmother, Dolores, is the ministry operations director. It has been obvious to me Danielle wants to be part of this ministry for the dying. I feel Danielle's presence there in the home is very strong. I believe she is continuing to serve God by praying for all those who are suffering and coming closer to their final days on this earth, especially those who are the loneliest, need the most love and whose hearts are the hardest.

After Danielle's death, I promised God He could give me as many children as he wanted, I would never complain again. God took me up on this promise and our family continued to grow and be blessed with many children. In August, 1995, the same year Danielle died, I became pregnant with our fifth child. We had our son, Jonathan Paul, born two months premature on 4 March 1996.

At birth, the doctor gave him a 50/50 chance for survival. He had to be left in the NICU for two weeks. The first week, we were not even allowed to hold him. As I struggled with my separation and endured watching Jonathan suffer, it brought back many memories of Danielle. After many prayers, especially prayers for Danielle's intercession, Jonathan's lungs stabilized and we brought him home. Before Jonathan was born, I had consecrated him to the Holy Spirit and he was baptized on Pentecost Sunday.

Our next child was a girl, Michaela Danielle, born on 17 August 1998. We were happy to give her Danielle's name. Then, 28 March 2001, we had a son, Patrick Gabriel. Like Jonathan, he was also born two months premature. This time, I had a severe case of Pre-eclampsia while I was pregnant and the doctors had to induce me two months early because of the threat to my life and to my baby's. We were blessed everything went well and Patrick was healthy and did not need to spend any time in the NICU.

We were gifted with two more daughters, Malia Regina, on 17 September 2005, which would have been Danielle's eighteenth birthday! It was beautiful knowing Malia shared a birthday with her big sister Danielle. Our last daughter was born, 24 January 2010. We named her, Isabelle Therese, after Danielle's favorite saint. Like Danielle, Isabelle also took the name of St. Therese for her Confirmation saint. Finally, our family was complete and we consider ourselves very blessed by God.

Our family has experienced many sufferings and joys. We feel both are blessings. He blessed us with suffering so we may have more opportunities to grow in our faith. Our sufferings have taught us to put our lives in God's hands and we must rely on Him and all His goodness. Besides suffering, we are equally as thankful for the joys God has given us. In the joys, we are able to experience God's love for us and just a small taste of the joy that awaits us when we are reunited together one day in Heaven.

As a mother, my greatest joy will be to one day stand before God, presenting all of my children to him for all eternity, just as I presented and consecrated each of them to His heart before they were born. That is my greatest desire and all I really want. I know the road will not be easy and I have already experienced many difficult paths, but I am ready to fight the good fight and with God's help, I have great hope we will achieve victory, for we belong to God.

Litany in Honor of the Little Therese

Lord, have mercy on us!
Christ, have mercy on us!
Lord, have mercy on us!
Christ, hear us!
Christ, graciously hear us!
God, the Father of Heaven, have mercy on us!
God, the son, Redeemer of the world, have mercy on us!
God, the Holy Spirit, have mercy on us!
Holy Trinity, one God, have mercy on us!
*Holy Mary, pray for us**
Holy Mother of God,
Holy Virgin of virgins,
Holy Therese of the Child Jesus,
Favored spouse of the Sovereign King,
Model of first communicants,
Lover of prayer,
Humble adorer of the Most Holy Eucharist,
Devout worshipper of the Sacred Heart of Jesus,
Faithful child of Mary,
Lily of chastity,
Rose of charity,

Violet of humility,
Model of obedience,
Lover of holy poverty,
Cheerful bearer of the cross,
Oblation for priests,
Patroness of Missions and Missionaries,
Ornament of the Carmelites,
Seraphic daughter of St. Teresa of Jesus,
Directress of little souls,
Wonderful advocate at the throne of God,
Refuge of the troubled and suffering,

*Pray for us, is repeated after each invocation.

Lamb of God, Who takes away the sins of the world, spare us, O Lord!
Lamb of God, Who takes away the sins of the world, graciously hears us, O Lord!
Lamb of God, who takes away the sins of the world, have mercy on us, O Lord!

V. Pray for us, St. Therese of the Child Jesus,
R. That we may be made worthy of the promises of Christ.

Let us pray

O Lord, who have said, Unless you become as little children, you shall not enter into the kingdom of heaven, grant us, we beseech You, so to follow the footsteps of Your virgin Therese in humility and simplicity of heart, that we may obtain the rewards of eternity. Who live and reign with

God the Father in the unity of the Holy Spirit, world without end. Amen.

TWENTY-FOUR GLORY BE TO THE FATHER'S NOVENA

To, Saint Therese of the Child Jesus and the Holy Face asking for necessary favors.

THE NOVENA

The twenty-four Glory Be to the Father's novena can be said at any time. However, the ninth to the seventeenth of the month is particularly recommended, for on those days the petitioner joins in prayer with all those making the novena.

Between the Glory Be's, say, "Saint Therese of the Child Jesus, pray for us."

St. Therese, the Little Flower, please pick
me a rose from the heavenly garden and send
it to me with a message of love. Ask God
to grant me the favor I thee implore and tell
Him I will love Him each day more and more.

The Twelve Promises of the Sacred Heart to St. Margaret Mary

Our Lord Jesus Christ made these twelve promises, to those who honor His Sacred Heart, to St. Margaret Mary Alacoque, a French nun, whom he called 'the Beloved Disciple of the Sacred Heart' and the Heiress 'of all its treasures', in the 1670s. They show us how much he cherishes this devotion. Considering that the blood that redeemed us at Calvary came from His Sacred Heart and that so much love and light still exude from it, these promises were revealed in one of many private revelations that Jesus gave St. Margaret Mary. Our Lord promised the following:

12 Promises of the Sacred Heart

1. I will give them all the graces necessary for their state of life.
2. I will establish peace in their families.
3. I will bless every home in which an image of My Heart is exposed and honored.
4. I will console them in all their difficulties.
5. I will be their refuge during life and especially at the hour of death.
6. I will shed abundant blessing upon all their undertakings.
7. Sinners shall find in My Heart a fountain and boundless ocean of mercy.
8. Tepid souls shall become fervent.
9. Fervent souls shall rise speedily to great perfection.

10. I will give to priests the power of touching the hardest hearts.

11. Those who propagate this devotion shall have their names written in My Heart never to be blotted out.

12. I promise you, in the excessive mercy of My Heart that My all-powerful love will grant to all who communicate on the first Friday of the month for nine consecutive months the grace of final penitence; they shall not die in My displeasure nor without their last Sacraments: 'My Divine Heart shall be their safe refuge in this last moment'.

+ Imprimatur: E Morrogh Bernard Vic Gen.,
Westmonasteril, 1954

Jesus promised St. Margaret Mary Alacoque that He *will bless the home in which the image of my Sacred Heart shall be exposed and honored.* When we place the image of the Sacred Heart of Jesus in a prominent place in our homes, we signify that Jesus is the King and the center and source of love for all.

You and your family are encouraged to learn, pray, and prepare your hearts for the Enthronement of the Sacred Heart in your home.